Wild Wings

THE HIDDEN WORLD OF BIRDS

MICHAEL RUNTZ

Wild Wings

THE HIDDEN WORLD OF BIRDS

ALSO FEATURING THE PHOTOGRAPHS OF JIM FLYNN

The BOSTON
MILLS PRESS

Canadian Cataloguing in Publication Data

Runtz, Michael W. P.

      Wild wings : the hidden world of birds

Includes index.

ISBN 1-55046-184-2

1. Birds. 2. Birds-Pictorial works I. Title.

QL673.R85 1996   598   C96-930706-3

Cover: *Great Blue Herons often fly great distances from feeding to nesting sites.*

Opposite title page: *Some seed-eaters, Pine Grosbeaks included, devour the pulp as well as the seeds of crab apples and other fruit.*

First published in 1996 by
The Boston Mills Press
132 Main Street
Erin, Ontario, Canada
N0B 1T0
(519) 833-2407 Fax (519) 833-2195

An affiliate of
Stoddart Publishing Co. Limited
34 Lesmill Road
North York, Ontario, Canada
M3B 2T6

The publisher gratefully acknowledges the support of the Canada Council and Ontario Arts Council in the development of writing and publishing in Canada.

Boston Mills Books are available for bulk purchase for sales promotions, premiums, fundraising, and seminars. For details, contact the *Special Sales Department,* Stoddart Publishing Co. Limited, at the address opposite.

Design by Andrew Smith
Copy-editing by Heather Lang-Runtz
Page composition by Andrew Smith Graphics Inc.
Printed in Hong Kong by Book Art Inc. Toronto.

To the memory of Adolf Vogg,
whose love for birds and all things wild was equalled only by his passion for
sharing his interests and knowledge with others.

When a Canada Goose lowers its neck to the ground, the bold chin strap breaks up its neck profile, rendering the bird less visible. This new chick obviously does not yet have either this feature or its mother's instinct.

INTRODUCTION

There is something magical about birds: they drift through the air like feathered spirits; their radiant colors delight the eye; and their exhilarating songs stir the soul.

I was smitten by birds at a very early age. My next-door neighbor, an amateur birdwatcher, used to lead me by the hand around her yard and show me orioles (known as Baltimores in those days) nesting in the majestic elms. For a five-year-old, it was magical to see a distant splash of color up close in binoculars and then match that image to one held in a book. Who would have predicted that this first exposure to birds, designed to keep a young brat from pestering his sister and her friend, would lead to a lifelong passion?

At first, I wanted only to identify every bird I encountered. I spent countless hours deciphering their spots, stripes, or other markings, and once my identification skills were honed, I became obsessed with adding new species to my lifelist. For many years a string of checkmarks beside a column of names reflected my sole interest in birds.

But the relentless drive to "list" began to wane as I discovered that the more I looked — not just glanced — the more my interest was captured by things other than their identities. I finally realized that there was more to birds than just identifiable flashes of colors and patterns. Behind the rich diversity of appearances existed a world of captivating behaviors. Inevitably, the whys and the hows came to dominate my interests, with field identification assuming a much reduced, secondary role.

Wild Wings: The Hidden World of Birds is by no means an identification guide; a number of other excellent publications fulfill this need quite nicely. Rather, this book is an introduction to the principles behind the myriad remarkable appearances and behaviors found in North American birds. I hope this book inspires you to explore the magical world of birds, and that you come away with more than a column of checkmarks beside a list of names!

With soft-edged feathers that silence their flight, dish-shaped faces that capture the slightest sound, light-gathering eyes that penetrate the deepest darkness, and razor-sharp talons that easily snare elusive prey, Great Gray Owls (opposite) and other members of their group are marvelously well adapted for their predatory lifestyle.

ACKNOWLEDGMENTS

I am compelled to begin by thanking the people responsible for starting me off in this wonderful hobby/career: my sister Karen and her friend Monique Baker, for complaining to Monique's mom about my playhouse antics; Monique's mom, Cecile, for distracting me by forcibly taking me around her yard and showing me those magical orioles nesting in the trees; Mr. R. T. Peterson, for putting the wonderful pictures of those orioles in his remarkable field guide; Bud Levy, Edna Ross, George Findlay, Adolf Vogg — dear friends who are no longer here to thank in person — and Sloan Watters for nurturing my budding interest in birds. To my countless birding comrades who kept my skills and pencils sharp, thanks for your companionship and generous sharing of knowledge. And to Jim Flynn (whose outstanding photos grace this book), Bob Graham, and Bill Reynolds, thanks for at least trying to show me which end of the camera to use.

A special thank you to Ron Pittaway and Pat (Dr. P. J.) Weatherhead for your critical reviews of this manuscript and for contributing in your own special ways to my enjoyment of birds.

In addition, I would like to thank A. Ron Wilson of Kodak Canada Inc. and Fumitaka Yamada of Canon Canada Inc. for their gracious support of my photographic endeavors.

And last but never least, to my wife, Heather, and my sons, Harrison and Dylan, thanks for understanding and supporting my never-ending disappearances into the natural world.

CONTENTS

Bathing helps to maintain feathers. Herring Gulls that feed in the ocean often bathe in nearby freshwater to get rid of the salt.

CHAPTER ONE

WINGS OF FREEDOM

From paintings on the walls of Stone Age caves to the popularity of today's birdwatching outings, humans have long demonstrated an appreciation for birds. Their brilliant colors, elegant displays, and freedom to roam the skies have won our hearts and captured our imagination. Amazingly, all these traits, which we have found so alluring, are based on a single avian feature, one that sets birds apart from all other animals.

The development of feathers was the impetus that sent birds down a distinct evolutionary path. Feathers gave to birds their identity — as a group, as species, and as individuals. By performing a number of discrete functions, they also enabled birds to become the most successful group of terrestrial vertebrates, inhabiting virtually every nook and cranny on this planet.

Color is not all show and no substance; the dark tips of the flight feathers of many birds, such as Crested Caracaras (opposite) and Herring Gulls (above), are more resistant to wear.

Feathers unquestionably enhance a bird's appearance. But their beauty does not lie in living material. Like hair, feathers emerge from follicles in the skin and are made of keratin, a fibrous substance resistant to microbe and fungi attacks. While the keratin found in the feathers and leg scales of birds is not identical to that found in today's reptiles, there is little doubt that feathers evolved from the scales of an early reptilian ancestor.

Over millions of years feathers have been refined into five main types, each with different functions. Contour feathers, which cover most of a bird's body, give the bird its streamlined shape and protect it from the damaging effects of the sun, vegetation, and abrasive particles in the air. A typical contour feather has a flat blade consisting of a vane on each side of a central support shaft, the rachis. Each vane consists of parallel branches, known as barbs, emanating from the rachis. From the barbs emerge smaller branches or barbules. Through a system of little hooks and ridges, the barbules interlock, and so lend strength and flexibility without adding weight. The afterfeather, a downy lower part of the vane found in many birds, provides insulation.

Birds use specially modified contour feathers to power them through the air. The large, stiff flight feathers located in the wings (remiges) and the tail (rectrices) are similar in structure to basic contour feathers but lack a downy base.

The vanes in wing flight feathers are asymmetrical, with the leading one narrower to cut air. By causing the feathers to twist when subjected to air pressure, this asymmetry enhances lift during flight. Special friction barbules on the outer (primary) wing feathers strengthen the wing by keeping overlying feathers together. While wing flight feathers provide power and control, those in the tail are used mainly for braking and steering.

With their loose tangle of hookless barbules, the fluffy down feathers trap air, creating a plush layer of insulation under the contour feathers. Semiplumes, intermediate in structure between down and contour feathers, also insulate, and in some birds — Great Egrets and Snowy Egrets, for example — have been modified into elegant display ornaments. Filoplumes, the hair-like feathers located next to contour and flight feathers, are sensitive to feather movement and pressure changes, and relay important information to the muscles that control feather position. Stiff, spiny feathers known as bristles perform a variety of sensory and protective functions. The bristles at the base of a woodpecker's bill, for example, keep dust and wood chips from entering the bird's nostrils when it is drilling into wood. The long bristles encircling the bills of Chuck-will's-widows, Common Poorwills, and other nightjars may help to detect flying insects as well as funnel them into the bird's open mouth.

Feathers not only give Green Herons (opposite) and other birds their great beauty, they also give them identity.

The thick down that covers young birds such as this juvenile Long-eared Owl provides them with much-needed warmth (opposite left). With the arrival of adulthood (opposite above) comes a remarkable change in appearance for this and most other species. The earth-toned colors in a Wilson's Phalarope's feathers (opposite below) are due to the presence of melanin pigments.

Feathers are an essential part of every bird. But they have long eclipsed their purely physical function. The near-infinite array of colors and patterns helps to conceal birds from the hungry eyes of a predator as well as make them dangerously obvious to a potential mate. The diverse colors that render birds as beautiful a group of animals as any other on land or in the sea originate from two sources.

Most colors result from pigments embedded in the barbs and barbules. Feathers that contain melanins, the pigments responsible for earth-toned colors, have a greater resistance to wear because of a high level of keratin. For that reason, gulls, terns, hawks, and other birds that spend considerable time in the air often possess melanin-rich black wing tips. The more vibrant colors are produced by lipochrome pigments, of which the most intense are often diet-related.

Other colors are caused by a feather's structural characteristics. Special hollow melanin granules (often modified into platelets or tubes) in the barbules directionally reflect incoming light rays. Light bouncing off as many as 15 layers of platelets stacked in flattened barbules is responsible for the luminous throat gorgets of hummingbirds. This brilliant iridescence as well as the colorful wing patches (specula) of ducks can only be seen when light is reflected at a specific angle. But this is not the case for other structural colors. The breathtaking blues of bluebirds and Indigo Buntings, for example, are caused by the scattering of light, not by pigmentation. Since the light striking minute melanin particles in the barbs is scattered in all directions, however, the colors are visible — no matter which way you look at the bird.

Function and color aside, feathers are impressive in terms of sheer numbers. A hummingbird sports about a thousand feathers, and this is on the low end of the scale. On the high end, a swan bears about 25,000! With so many feathers playing a number of essential roles, it is crucial that they be in good repair. Feather care is a daily necessity, with some birds attending to this task every hour.

Birds are equipped with all the necessary tools for complete grooming. The beak is used to preen every feather except those beyond reach on the head and upper neck. During preening, the beak can be wiped over the feathers, or individual feathers can be drawn through it while the bird gently nibbles. Preening restores the structural integrity of the feathers, removes dirt and parasites, and distributes protective secretions produced in a gland on the rump. The preen or uropygial gland, located above the base of the upper tail feathers, releases an oily mixture of waxes, fats, and fatty acids. These secretions not only lubricate the feathers, keeping them pliable and making them more resistant to water, bacteria, fungi, and parasites, but also help to maintain the bill. Herons produce another waterproofing agent, derived from special down feathers called powderdown that are scattered among the contour feathers. Unlike preen gland secretions, however, the keratin particles released by the powderdown are dry and resemble talcum powder.

The vibrant reds and yellows of a male Yellow-bellied Sapsucker (above) are caused by lipochrome pigments, some of which are diet-related. It is unfortunate that some of the most striking colors, such as those in the gorgets of Anna's Hummingbirds (opposite) and others in this group, are not always on display. As a result of the feathers' structure, the stunning iridescence can only be viewed from certain angles.

For areas that the bill cannot reach, grooming takes the form of scratching with the feet, either by holding the leg under or over a wing. Ground-dwelling warblers tend to use the under-the-wing technique, while their arboreal relatives generally prefer the over-the-wing method. No matter how scratching is executed, however, preen gland secretions are first picked up by rubbing the bill over the preen gland and then passing the feet over the bill. A number of birds take scratching one step forward, so to speak. A comb-like ridge on the middle toes of herons, nightjars, and Barn Owls actually augments their feather grooming efforts, particularly when it comes to removing unwanted parasites.

Several rather unusual behaviors can be ascribed to feather care. Many songbirds, including Northern Flickers and Blue Jays, snatch ants in their bills, then stroke the displeased insects through their feathers. American Crows will squat over an ant hill with their wings and tail spread, deliberately enticing the angry ants to swarm through their plumage. One possible reason for such "ant-ics" is that the chemicals (usually formic acid) released by the distressed ants repel feather and skin parasites and discourage bacterial and fungal intrusions.

Bathing is another important hygienic ritual. Besides cleansing the bird, baths keep feathers pliable and may be important in distributing preen oils more evenly through the plumage. Humans bathe in many different ways (some preferring showers; others taking sponge baths; still others spending hours nearly submerged in a tub); so too do birds. American Robins, Northern Mockingbirds, and other strong-legged birds wade into puddles, quickly dunk their bellies and dip their heads, and splash with their wings. Small birds such as warblers and wrens dash in and out of shallow water, immersing themselves, and even rolling completely over. Flycatchers dive right in from an elevated perch. Swallows and swifts bathe on the wing by dipping into the water during flight. And a few birds, including woodpeckers, prefer simply to spread their wings open in the rain. Bathing is not limited to the warm seasons: on sunny winter days, open water attracts a variety of birds, while a few even choose to bathe right in the snow.

After coming out of the water, birds often "catch a few rays," exposing their feathers to the sun. The feathers are usually shaken vigorously before a brief drying period, followed by preening. For birds with poorly waterproofed feathers and less developed preen glands — cormorants, for example — sunbathing, or sunning, is important for drying soaked feathers. The wings are held open in direct sunlight for long periods of time. Anhingas spend much time perched with wings and tail spread open and directed towards the sun, as do cormorants. This posture was initially thought to be designed primarily to dry wet feathers (Anhingas also have poorly developed preen glands), but now it is believed that their feather structure prevents severe wetting and that sunbathing is performed more as a means of thermoregulation. In fact, many birds bask to absorb solar energy, particularly in cold weather. Sunning is also important for feather maintenance, as the ultraviolet component of sunlight may trigger the synthesis of vitamin D when it comes into contact with the preen oils and other components of the skin and feathers. And the heat of the sun may drive parasites into sites more easily accessed during grooming.

Feather wear can be to a bird's advantage. By sporting pale-tipped feathers to its winter dress, a European Starling (left) does not need to expend the energy required to molt in new breeding plumage. As the pale ends wear away, by spring, the resplendent nuptial coat shines through.
An absence of certain pigments creates unusual appearances in common birds. This American Robin (right), not fully an albino, managed to survive to adulthood, a feat not always accomplished by a bird so obvious to predators.

Feather grooming is an integral part of the daily routine of
American Black Ducks (above) and all other birds.
Many birds, including this Anhinga (right), draw their feathers
through their bills to repair and clean them.

Snowy Egrets and other herons groom their head and neck feathers with a unique tool located on one toe of each foot (opposite).
The toe comb is particularly useful in extracting feather parasites from sites their bills cannot reach (below).

Although many birds take to the water to cleanse their feathers, others bathe in quite dry sites. Dust bathing or "dusting" may help House Sparrows, grouse, and birds that live in arid regions to get rid of excess oils and control feather lice and other parasites.

Grooming, bathing, and sunning — despite ongoing feather maintenance, daily exposure to the physical surroundings and changes in the weather take their toll. Worn feathers that fail to do their job must be replaced, and so most adult birds molt or replace their feathers at least once a year. Many have two molts, the second being partial only. Because considerable energy is expended to replace feathers, molting rarely occurs in periods when the energy drain is high, such as the nesting season and migration. Many birds lose and replace their feathers gradually and systematically without affecting their ability to fly, yet loons, waterfowl, and a few other aquatic birds tend to lose them all at once. During these "complete overhauls," the birds are flightless and vulnerable; waterfowl become exceedingly secretive.

Although molting keeps a bird clothed in fresh, fully functional feathers, it has another important function. It enables most species to sport conspicuous courtship garb in one season and a drab, cryptic coat in another. The few species that do not molt before the breeding season — European Starlings, House Sparrows, and Snow Buntings, for example — exhibit striking plumage changes nonetheless. But feather wear, not molt, is responsible for this magical change. The winter feathers of these birds have pale edges that continually wear throughout that season. By spring the wear unmasks striking colors that were previously concealed. European Starlings go through a particularly dramatic transformation, changing from dull, spotted birds in winter to shiny, sleek birds with dazzling purple-and-green iridescence glowing through all their black spring plumage.

Feathers do more than define birds as a group. They give birds shape and form. They hide them from prying eyes and protect them from the elements. They endow them with colors that intimidate unwanted rivals and impress potential mates. They enable some birds to produce sound; others to better detect it. And, by transforming simple appendages into wings of freedom, they have liberated birds from the shackles that tie most other animals to an earthbound existence.

When bathing, small birds such as this Nashville Warbler (opposite) prefer quick dips and even roll over to wet their backs. Anhingas (below) lack developed preen glands and the waterproofing oil of most birds, but their feather structure keeps their feathers from becoming waterlogged. Frequent sunbathing may serve more to keep the birds warm and to help rid the feathers of parasites.

CHAPTER TWO

BIRDS OF A FEATHER

In a moment of poetic reflection, have you ever longed to live the carefree life of a bird? To soar freely high above the earth? To carol in the new day while basking in the warmth of the rising sun? Well, a day or two spent under a coat of feathers would quickly dispel such romantic yearnings, for danger lurks in the sky above, on the ground below, and even in the still waters of quiet lakes and ponds. It would soon be apparent that nervous vigilance, not idyllic bliss, occupies much of a bird's waking moments.

A bird's eye placement is a compromise between the need to find food and the need to detect danger.
To see more of the environment at any one moment, songbirds such as American Robins (above) have their eyes on
the sides of their heads. Birds of prey have eyes located more frontally for better depth perception.
By flocking, birds can spend more time feeding than looking for predators, because of a more-eyes principle. Bohemian Waxwings
(opposite) are able to travel in single-species flocks because their food is found in large, easily shared quantities.

To stay alive, a bird must always keep its eye open, always on the lookout for predators. Because each eye possesses a separate field of view, two eyes offer even better coverage of a bird's surroundings. This coverage is maximized because the eyes are located on the sides, not the front, of a bird's head. With their lateral eye placement, Rock Doves enjoy an impressive 300 degrees of viewing area. American Woodcocks have almost 360 degrees of coverage because their eyes are situated toward the back of the head. The benefits of this unusual placement become especially apparent when this odd-looking bird is feeding. With its bill probing into the soft ground for worms, a woodcock's eyes appear to lie near the "top" of its head. In this position the woodcock is able to survey the area ahead, above, and behind, simultaneously.

Most other birds, however, would go hungry if their eyes were placed similarly to those of a woodcock. Woodcocks don't need to see their food to catch it — their beaks encounter it randomly — but other birds have to locate their food visually and judge its distance before they can pick it up. The ability to perceive distances is created by an overlap of each eye's field of view, an overlap that is virtually nonexistent in a woodcock. As the eyes are moved forward, the degree of overlap increases, as does the resulting binocular vision or depth perception. But an increase in depth perception comes at a price: with both fields of view shifting forward, the total field of view decreases, producing a large blind spot behind the head. A bird compensates for this by periodically ceasing to feed and moving its head to scan its surroundings.

For most birds, a delicate balance must be struck between the amount of time spent foraging for food and looking out for danger. During the nesting season, when food is plentiful and discrete territories have been established, most birds forage alone. But during migration or in the winter, when food is scarce and exposure to predators increases, most birds find it more advantageous to travel and feed in flocks. Each member of the flock is able to spend less time on guard and more time foraging because the group as a whole is constantly vigilant. Another benefit to flocking originates from a safety-in-numbers principle. If a predator were to strike, the odds are improved that any one individual would escape. En route to new feeding or roosting sites, flocks are often fairly loosely structured. Should a predator appear, the birds quickly tighten up their formation. Whirling and wheeling, the compact flock reacts as a synchronized, precisely choreographed unit, making it difficult for a predator to single out a potential target. Should it detect a bird that is physically disadvantaged or displays poor judgment and deviates from the flock's flight plan, however, the hunter's response is swift.

When threatened, a flock of Semipalmated Sandpipers (opposite) transforms from a loosely structured group into a well-synchronized corps, wheeling and turning as if it were a single entity.

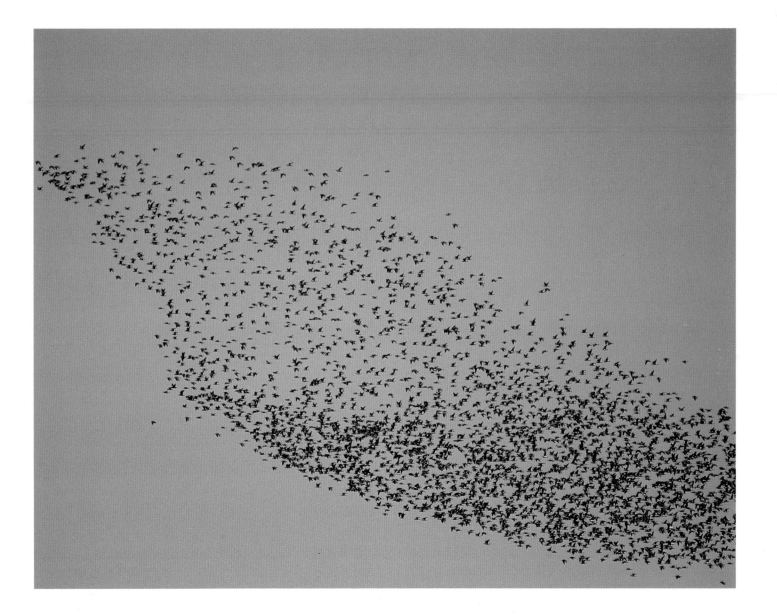

Many ground-nesting birds almost perfectly mimic their environment. Whip-poor-wills (below left), American Woodcocks (below right), and female Spruce Grouse (opposite) bear the colors and patterns that dominate in their habitat.

The old saying "birds of a feather flock together" applies quite nicely to the defensive behavior of waterfowl, shorebirds, waxwings, and northern finches, birds that commonly travel in single-species flocks. But other birds, particularly migrating warblers and sparrows, travel in mixed-species flocks, and mixed bands of birds roam the winter woodlands.

The difference in flocking behavior arises from the one major drawback to flocking. As the number of hungry mouths increases, so too does the competition for food. In a single-species flock, every member competes for the same resource, using the same methods — which isn't a problem as long as the food is found in large quantities over a wide area. When a couple of dozen Bohemian Waxwings descend on a berry-laden Mountain-ash tree, each bird is able to find enough to eat without aggressively fighting over individual berries. A rich coastal bay yields enough molluscs to keep a flock of even 100 White-winged Scoters from stealing from one another. But there comes a time when group size becomes a hindrance. When the flock is so large that members crowd each other and fight over food and space, energy is wasted. Because of all the squabbling, total vigilance is lost and the risk of being caught off guard rises.

While a large flock may not always be ideal, a small flock can also be disadvantageous. Birds in small flocks tend to be more nervous, scanning frequently; they waste energy reacting to false alarms. The optimal size of a flock is achieved only when aggressive interaction among individuals has been minimized and vigilance is maintained even though each member spends more time feeding than watching.

But not all foods are available in quantities large enough to support a single-species flock. Dormant insects and spiders, for example, are seldom found in dense concentrations. A flock of a dozen White-breasted Nuthatches or Downy Woodpeckers would be hard-pressed to find enough food in most woodlots. But what if a couple of nuthatches and one or two woodpeckers were to travel with a half-dozen Black-capped Chickadees and a Brown Creeper? There would be less competition for specific food items because each species uses a different foraging method: nuthatches search crevices from an upside-down position; creepers work a tree in an upward spiral, probing sideways under the bark; chickadees dig into shallow crevices and punky wood; and woodpeckers chip off the bark. Yet, every member of this heterogeneous flock benefits from increased vigilance because of the more-eyes principle. During the fall and winter, if certain food resources are found in small, scattered clumps, mixed-species flocks tend to prevail.

Even when not feeding, birds face the risk of a predatory attack. By remaining motionless and blending into the background with the aid of camouflage, birds at rest avoid detection. Earth-toned feathers punctuated and patterned with spots and streaks render ground-nesting birds such as Common Poorwills, Whip-poor-wills, American Woodcocks, and Ruffed Grouse almost invisible. Quite possibly your heart has leapt into your throat when one of these hidden birds has exploded out from almost underfoot! The shock effect of this noisy departure holds real meaning in a predator – prey context. By startling an intruder for even a moment, the bird might extend its life to at least one more encounter.

Patterns and colors that match a bird's background help to hide it from a predator's eyes. When an American Bittern points its bill to the sky and freezes, the stripes on its breast allow it to vanish among the reeds. Other markings conceal the bird in quite a different way. The bold breast bands of a Killdeer or a Horned Lark, as well as the eyestripe on a songbird's head protruding above a nest, make the bird difficult to spot by breaking up or disrupting the bird's general configuration. Wing bars and tail bands may well serve the same function.

Any form of camouflage serves its purpose only when a bird remains motionless. Whenever a predator appears, birds often "freeze," counting on their special patterns to render them invisible. Ironically, the very patterns that are designed to make birds disappear are often the very markings used by humans to distinguish between species.

It may be more than just coincidence that so many birds are dark above and pale below. Since the upper parts shade the belly, this contrast in colors may help to lessen the shading effect. Because a three-dimensional appearance stands out more strongly from a background, the more uniform or "flatter" appearance created by the "countershading" coloration may actually allow a bird to blend better into its surroundings.

Even at night, sleeping birds are never completely safe from a predator's grasp. Although solitary birds will often roost in secluded sites, European Starlings, blackbirds, swallows, herons, and vultures roost in large groups. Communal roosts may be energy-efficient or may serve as information centers for

Patterns often allow a bird to vanish into its background.
The breast stripes of a motionless American Bittern, its bill pointed to the sky, enable the bird to blend in with the vertical vegetation around it.
Even when there is no cover, a bittern will still freeze, demonstrating that this behavior is a far-from-intelligent act.

Killdeer breast bands and other conspicuous markings are often designed to break up a bird's outline, making it hard to see from ground level (below). Eye and head stripes can serve as disruptive patterns for Chipping Sparrows (opposite) and other nesting birds whose heads project above a nest when the birds are incubating.

food-finding. Also, the birds gain advantage from a safety-in-numbers principle, for the more birds there are, the less chance of an individual being captured during a predator's visit.

"A good offense may be the best defense" aptly describes the defensive strategy adopted by some birds. When cornered out of its nest, a young Great Horned Owl will put on a fearsome performance. With feathers fluffed and wings spread, the young owl looks twice its size as it hisses and clacks its beak at the intruder. If this display fails to persuade the predator to seek an easier meal, a rake of the owl's razor-sharp claws may be more convincing.

Rather than hide when a predator is spotted, many birds will actually approach it. When an American Crow spots an adult Great Horned Owl roosting in a tree, its angry calls soon summon others to its find. Within minutes, a screaming black mob descends upon the owl. It is only a matter of time until the owl, fed up with the relentless stream of verbal and physical abuse, seeks a quieter retreat. Smaller owls and other predators, such as weasels and snakes, frequently elicit similar responses from songbirds. In these cases, however, a number of birds (often a mixture of chickadees, nuthatches, thrushes, vireos, and warblers) react to the alarm calls of a bird in distress. The calls of other birds responding to the initial alarm entice still more to join the mob. The growing mob usually continues to harass the predator until it moves on (the common result) or the group loses interest. At first glance, it might seem foolish for a bird to approach a predator. Why would a bird not head for deeper cover upon hearing the alarm calls of

Many nesting waterbirds, including Common Loons (opposite), lower their heads to obscure their distinctive outlines. The "necklace" and the back spots also help to make the bird disappear from sight. (Below) A good offense may sometimes be the best defense. Although this American Crow has little to fear from the Osprey, like many other birds, it reacts aggressively when encountering a raptor and usually attracts other mobbers in the process.

another? After all, would it not be more prudent to slip away and hide? Despite the apparent paradox, there may well be a number of benefits to mobbing. Quite possibly the predator will be driven off by the group effort, making the area safe for the mobbing birds as well as for their offspring. Or, as the participating birds learn exactly where the danger lies, the predator loses the element of surprise. If the birds hid, the predator could still mount a surprise attack.

Birds most often mob during the breeding season or in areas where resident birds, such as Black-capped Chickadees, hold territories all year. And, because they have nothing to gain by driving a predator away from an area they will not be using for nesting purposes, migrating birds are less inclined to mob than territorial birds. Thus, it seems that the primary benefit of mobbing is to make a territory safer for a bird and its young, not to identify the location of a predator.

For predator and prey alike, every day is a struggle for survival. Nature is unforgiving, and those who fail to remain alert seldom live long. Even for those who successfully evade the army of hungry mouths, other hazards lie ahead. A bird's environment can impose hardships as potentially deadly as the attack of any skilled predator.

Chapter Three

ELEMENTARY SOLUTIONS

When a summer's sky is a bottomless blue and the wind fails to muster even a whisper, the day is often referred to as "a bluebird kind of day." Unfortunately, for those who have bluebirds in their neighborhood, these colorful birds possess no special relationship with the elements. Inclement weather is as much a part of their world as it is ours. From season to season and often on a daily basis, birds must cope with drastic changes in climate. The ability to overcome scorching heat and killing cold, severe drought and torrential rains has enabled birds to inhabit all major habitats of the world.

On cool mornings, Greater Roadrunners (above) save energy by basking. Typically, they raise the back feathers to expose their dark bases and aim them towards the sun. Many finches, this Purple Finch (opposite) included, often winter in relatively cold regions. They stay warm by increasing their feather mass before the onset of winter, by raising their feathers to trap air, and by shivering frequently.

On hot days, Eastern Kingbirds (below left) and other small birds cool off by panting to increase the rate of evaporative cooling. Although this bird cannot seek a shady retreat because of its nestlings, it is at least able to provide shade for them. Water cools birds as well as cleans them. On extremely hot days, Killdeers (below right) extend the cooling effects of water to their eggs by wetting their bellies.

The success of birds stems from their feathers, but not just because they empower birds with flight. Feathers, by their structure and placement, also protect a bird from environmental adversity. Growing from small pits called follicles, feathers are grouped in concentrations called tracts. Elaborate bands of tiny muscles linking the follicles raise, lower, and turn the feathers, often in response to stimuli received by the filoplumes.

The position of the feathers dramatically affects the rate at which body heat is lost or retained. On hot days, feathers are pulled tight against the body, and blood vessels next to the skin dilate to increase the blood flow. Heat released from the blood passes through compressed feathers at a much faster rate than when the feathers are raised, so by becoming sleeker a bird also becomes cooler. As white is a better solar energy reflector than black, one might expect birds living in hot regions to be primarily pale-plumaged, yet a number of birds that inhabit arid regions are quite dark, and a few — Phainopeplas, Chihuahuan Ravens, and Black-billed Magpies, for example — are largely black.

Obviously, there is more to the relationship between feather color and thermal benefit than just solar reflectance. Dark plumage conducts body heat more readily than does white, and under windy conditions it absorbs less solar energy. A bird's color is also influenced by the need for camouflage and other factors, including the level of humidity. With all these different forces at work, there is never one perfect appearance for any given habitat.

While most body feathers are pulled in to facilitate heat loss, others are fluffed out. By raising overlying feathers, bare tracts of skin, such as those located on the head, back, and under the bend of the wing, are exposed to the air. These sites lose more heat when they are directed into the wind.

While Burrowing Owls and many other birds that inhabit arid regions are pale,
some are dark, a few even black. Light-colored feathers may absorb less solar energy on calm days than do dark feathers,
but on windy days they actually absorb more.

The lanky legs of Great Blue Herons (below) provide an excellent means of releasing excess heat on hot days.
Blood flow in these extremities can be regulated so that less heat is lost in cold weather. While standing in water accelerates a bird's heat loss,
Wood Storks (opposite) also defecate on their legs to rid their body of excess heat through evaporative cooling.

Air cooling alone is not enough to keep a bird comfortable on really hot days. Even though birds lack sweat glands, water evaporation is still an essential means of getting rid of excess heat. Most of the evaporation occurs in the respiratory tract. When songbirds open their beaks and pant, the evaporation rate is hastened as the amount of air flowing over the moist surfaces of their mouth, pharynx, bronchi, and possibly even the air sacs is increased. Non-passerines such as owls, herons, and boobies regulate the rate of evaporation by rapidly oscillating their throats. This odd behavior is known as "gular fluttering."

Heat can also be released in other body regions. Because of their lack of feathers, legs and feet are prime locations for this process. To accelerate heat loss, herons, gulls, and other large-footed, long-legged waterbirds increase the volume of warm blood flowing through these extremities. Standing maximizes the area of leg exposed and amplifies the amount of heat that is discharged. Standing in water yields even better results. But some birds achieve this without the aid of water. By defecating on their legs, Black Vultures, Wood Storks, and Turkey Vultures increase their rate of evaporative cooling.

Behavior also plays a role in beating the heat. When the sun overhead burns with sweltering intensity, many birds retire to cool, shady areas. A large number of songbirds find relief in the branches of leafy trees, while Rock Wrens, true to their name, scurry into rocky crevices. But instead of seeking shelter, some birds do the opposite and take to the skies. Birds of prey can often be seen soaring high overhead in the heat of the day. Even though they are exposed to the sun, these birds

After a cold night, a Ruffed Grouse (opposite left) thermoregulates by basking in a sheltered nook. In winter, most birds sleep in sheltered sites; a few under the snow. Eastern Screech-Owls (opposite right) take advantage of the superior thermal properties of tree cavities by roosting in them year-round, commonly basking in their "lobbies" on cold days.

stay cool because lower temperatures prevail at high altitudes.

While raptors soar high above them, most birds rest during the hottest part of the day because activity generates heat. Even when a bird is resting, however, some heat is produced by its internal metabolism. For this reason, desert birds such as Common Poorwills often exhibit a lower metabolic rate than birds living in cooler regions.

Solutions to any problem embrace some risk, but one adaptation to excessive heat nudges that fine line separating life from death. While body temperatures above 115 degrees Fahrenheit (46 degrees Celsius) are usually fatal, a number of desert birds, including Mourning Doves living in the American southwest, allow their internal temperatures to climb to 113 degrees (45 degrees). By entering a controlled state of hyperthermia, the bird's temperature remains higher than that of its surroundings. As long as the ambient temperature does not climb above 113 degrees, the temperature gradient favors the flow of heat from the bird into its environment.

While birds living in southern regions have to contend with scorching heat, those that inhabit northern expanses are challenged by frigid temperatures. Here as well, feathers contribute to a bird's ability to survive. Just as we throw on additional layers of clothing, many birds grow more feathers to keep out the chill. In preparation for winter, American Goldfinches, Common Redpolls, and other finches increase their feather mass by as much as 50 percent. By fluffing its feathers and trapping air, a bird virtually doubles its insulation value and can reduce its heat loss by as much as a third. The feather coat is incredibly effective in keeping a bird warm: a difference of as much as 104 degrees Fahrenheit (40 degrees Celsius) can exist across a mere half an inch (1.5 centimeters) of feather insulation on a Black-capped Chickadee!

Feather color also helps to keep some birds warm. Since white feathers retain body heat and, in strong winds, absorb radiant heat better than dark plumage, Snowy Owls, Glaucous Gulls, winter ptarmigan, and other birds living in the Far North realize a thermal advantage from their white plumage.

Despite their importance as insulation, feathers do lose heat steadily to the environment. To replace this loss — and to prevent their internal temperatures from falling to fatal levels — birds must generate heat. While subcutaneous fat (fat stored under the skin) provides a certain degree of insulation in some animals, its main purpose in birds is to fuel the heat production process. Fat stores can be used up rather quickly; just one extremely cold night can deplete nearly all of a chickadee's reserves. If the fat stores are not replenished before the next cold night, the bird will freeze. This is why Evening Grosbeaks, Common Redpolls, and other northern finches often feed heavily just before heading off to roost. The food is held in the crop and gradually digested throughout the night to supplement the burning of their fat.

In keeping a bird warm, most of the fuel is used to fire up the massive flight or pectoral muscles. Oddly though, the heat is not usually generated by flying. Rather, it is muscle movement associated with shivering that creates the heat required to fend off the cold. While shivering can occur in bursts if milder conditions prevail, it increases in intensity and frequency when

the temperature drops. Many birds will shiver right through a cold night, and in northern areas locked in persistent cold, Common Ravens and other birds may shiver all winter long.

For those body parts that cannot be warmed by shivering or are not endowed with feathers, a bird's posture can be important in providing warmth. Roosting birds often tuck their head under their scapular feathers and pull one leg up into the breast feathers. When that leg is sufficiently warmed, it is switched with the other. Other birds cover both legs simultaneously by sitting on them. Juncos and American Tree Sparrows often plunk down while feeding, clothing their legs and feet with an insulating blanket of feathers.

But feet and legs cannot always be pulled in from the cold. Ducks and gulls often stand on ice or swim in frigid water for extended periods of time, and show no ill effects. This amazing feat (no pun intended) is achieved through an intricate heat exchange system known as the rete mirabile ("wonderful net"). The net is formed by arteries and veins elaborately branching and intertwining in the base of the leg. In the net, the opposing vessels are in such close proximity that heat is transferred from the 104-degrees-Fahrenheit (40 degrees Celsius) arterial blood to the cold 40-degrees-Fahrenheit (about 4 degrees Celsius) venous blood returning to the body. This transfer, known as counter-current exchange, cools the blood arriving at the foot to about 43 degrees Fahrenheit (6 degrees Celsius). A cool foot loses less heat than a hot one, and since heat equates with energy, both are conserved by this exchange. And by restricting the amount of blood reaching the outer parts of the

foot, heat loss is reduced further. When the smaller, outer blood vessels of the foot constrict, much of the arterial blood arriving at the base of the foot is shunted directly into the vein returning to the body, bypassing much of the foot's extremities, where valuable heat would be lost.

Staying warm during a winter's day is usually less of a challenge than surviving a long, frigid night. By choosing a favorable roosting site, however, birds can greatly improve the odds of greeting another sunrise. As the day ends, many birds disappear into the thick cover of coniferous trees. The dense foliage, especially when it is covered with snow, provides warmth in two ways: it blocks heat-stealing wind and traps some of the heat escaping from a sleeping bird. Even cosier, tree cavities are used as roosting sites by a variety of birds, including nuthatches, woodpeckers, chickadees, and small owls. While many birds shelter high above the snow, Ruffed Grouse, Common Redpolls, and Snow Buntings bury themselves right in the white stuff — giving legitimacy to the phrase "a blanket of snow."

Most birds struggle to maintain a high, constant body temperature, but a few do just the opposite. In cold weather, some birds deliberately lower their metabolism and allow their body temperature to drop. Turkey Vultures can lower their temperature by about 11 degrees Fahrenheit (6 degrees Celsius); other birds experience a more dramatic drop.

Hummingbirds allow their body temperatures to fall by as much as 36 degrees Fahrenheit (20 degrees Celsius), entering an inactive hypothermic state known as torpor. This ability to

One of the most northern birds in the world, Ivory Gulls (below) keep warm because of several adaptations. Their white plumage is better for retaining heat than are dark feathers, and actually absorbs more solar energy in windy conditions, which are common in the North.
Short black legs absorb solar energy and lose relatively less heat than long legs. And an amazing heat exchanger in the legs prevents the legs and feet from freezing, even when standing on ice or in frigid water.

dramatically lower body temperature is also developed in Black-capped Chickadees. These amazing birds can drop their internal temperatures by 22 degrees Fahrenheit (12 degrees Celsius). When overnight temperatures fall to only 32 degrees Fahrenheit (0 degrees Celsius) — a rather balmy condition for any northern region — almost 25 percent of the energy needed to maintain a chickadee's normal body temperatures is conserved. Because their small size is conducive to a high rate of heat loss, and because their diet of mainly insects and other small animals is fat-poor, chickadees tread an ecological tightrope every cold night. Unquestionably, the winter survival of these endearing birds is tightly linked to their ability to become torpid and conserve precious energy that would otherwise be used to maintain higher body temperatures.

Torpor is mainly a feature of small birds, for a larger bird would require just too much energy and time to bring its body temperature back to a normal level. The one exception is the Common Poorwill. These southwestern goatsuckers can stay lethargic for weeks, even months, at a time. During this prolonged hibernation (which gave rise to their Hopi Indian name "the sleeping one"), a poorwill's temperature can drop to 41 degrees Fahrenheit (5 degrees Celsius). Poorwills can also enter shorter periods of torpor during cold, wet periods in spring and summer, when heat loss is great and insects are hard to find.

Through a variety of physical and physiological adaptations, birds have overcome most environmental obstacles. Whether a desert parched by the scorching sun or a boreal forest locked in winter's icy grip, even the most challenging region is home to not one but a number of species. Yet the best-equipped bird is never guaranteed survival, for without adequate food, all adaptations for fending off environmental adversity are of little consequence.

CHAPTER FOUR

CONSUMING WAYS

Birds are feathered dynamos, endlessly flitting and fluttering, diving and darting. Whether evading deadly clutches and stuffing hungry mouths or fending off bitter cold and performing great sojourns, birds require enormous stores of energy. To keep their internal engines well-stoked, birds spend considerable time searching for food.

Whether it is an Atlantic Puffin (above) gathering a load of fish for its young or a woodpecker digging a beetle grub out of a branch, all birds must weigh the time and energy spent in getting the food against the return it yields. Any bird that overspends its budget faces the most severe penalty of all. Cedar Waxwings (opposite) and other specialized fruit-eaters have wide gapes for swallowing berries whole. Digesting only the pulp, the birds pass the seeds in their droppings, thereby acting as important dispersal agents.

House Finches (opposite) are seed-predators who crush the tough seed coats in their vice-like bills.

This quest involves energy and risk, as well. When foraging, birds must instinctively weigh the cost and danger of obtaining the food against the return that it yields. A bird whose meal provides less energy than the amount expended in getting it or who feeds in sites exposed to predators will not survive long. And so necessity, not random choice, has forced birds to forage in a fashion that maximizes their returns. The Northwestern Crow demonstrates this principle well. These small beachcombing crows feed on large marine snails called whelks, which they smash open by dropping them from the air. The birds optimize their net gains by selecting the largest whelks and dropping them from about 17 feet (5.2 meters), the minimum height at which most of the shells crack open. Smaller whelks are generally ignored because of their lower food value. And greater heights, though they may result in more smashed snails, are not flown to because of the considerable additional energy needed to reach them. Thus, these birds forage in a manner that gives them the highest return for their efforts.

But birds do not always seem to adopt the most energy-wise strategy; the rules are altered as needs change. When food resources are scarce, an underfed bird is more likely to gamble and take risks when foraging, or to select foods that offer poor returns.

Birds exploit a great variety of foods, but what is caviar to one species may be unpalatable fare to another. Even when several species share a common food source, there is a great deal of specialization both in the specific portions that are selected and in the way they are processed. Insects, for example, are eaten by a large number of birds. Flycatchers snatch flies from the air, woodpeckers dig beetle grubs out of wood, sandpipers extract maggots from the mud, and warblers pick caterpillars from the foliage. Such a general foraging breakdown can be further refined by looking at any one of these avian groups. Among woodpeckers, Hairy Woodpeckers chisel grubs from rotten limbs; Yellow-bellied Sapsuckers lap up small flies stuck in flowing tree sap; Northern Flickers pluck ants from their hills; Black-backed Woodpeckers devour bark beetles on spruce trunks stripped of their bark; and Red-headed Woodpeckers, behaving like flycatchers, seize grasshoppers on the wing. This partitioning of resources reduces competition among different birds, enabling a variety of species, including those closely related, to co-inhabit the same area.

While their diets may differ somewhat from ours, the nutritional requirements of birds are basically the same as that of humans. Fats and carbohydrates are necessary to produce energy, and proteins are needed to maintain and produce physical structures, tissues, and enzymes. To satisfy these needs, most birds eat a variety of foods, with many switching from animal prey (especially insects and spiders) to plant components (such as berries) during different seasons.

Although no one bird is a strict vegetarian, a range of species feeds on plants. Canada Geese graze the tender shoots of grasses, while Tundra Swans feast on the roots of Wild Celery. Ring-necked Pheasants and other gallinaceous birds consume an astounding variety of buds, seeds, and fruit; Ruffed Grouse, alone, exploit nearly 400 species of plants! A few birds

While woodpeckers are often considered to be mainly insectivores, Red-headed Woodpeckers (below) and a few other species also regularly dine on various fruits, including sumach drupes. Competition between seed-predators is reduced due to the birds' diversity of bill sizes and corresponding seed specializations. With their tiny bills, American Goldfinches (opposite top) delight in devouring the small seeds of thistles and other wildflowers. Birds that feed on nectar, such as this female Broad-billed Hummingbird (opposite bottom), seldom need to drink water, as their sugar-rich diet contains plenty of that liquid.

even eat the fully-developed leaves of trees and shrubs. The hardy Spruce Grouse thrives on a diet largely composed of Black Spruce, Larch, and Jack Pine needles.

It may appear that fruit and seeds are similar fare, but such is not the case. Fruits, which are loaded with carbohydrates, are succulent and easily digested but as a rule contain little protein and fat. Seeds, on the other hand, may contain higher levels of protein and fat but are protected by coats that are nearly impenetrable. Thrushes, waxwings, and other fruit-eaters are interested only in the sweet, soft pulp surrounding the seeds. By expelling the seeds, these birds play important roles as dispersers. Finches and other seed-eaters, on the other hand, destroy rather than disperse the seeds.

Fruit-eaters voraciously devour large amounts of pulp to acquire sufficient nutrition. Some eat double or even triple their own weight in a single day. To speed up the intake of food, birds usually swallow berries whole, a feat made possible by a large mouth opening, or gape. Bohemian Waxwings, which are more fruit-dependent than most birds, have gapes as wide as those found in birds twice their body mass. Fruit-eaters also have short intestines for faster processing of the material. Fruit can be digested amazingly quickly; it can take a Phainopepla a mere 12 minutes from the time a Mistle-toe berry is swallowed until its seeds are excreted!

Shorebirds, whose bills are specialized for extracting only certain types of food, display a tremendous partitioning of invertebrate resources. The massive beaks of Hudsonian Godwits (below left) are useful for digging deep for lugworms. With their fine tools, Least Sandpipers (below right) probe shallow mud for smaller prey. The massive bills of Pileated Woodpeckers (opposite) gain them access to the deep galleries of Carpenter Ants, and their amazingly long, sticky tongues pluck the insects from their most hidden recesses. Thick bristle feathers at the base of the beak prevent wood chips and dust from entering the nostrils.

Before dining on the nutritious inner core of a seed, seed-eaters have one tough problem to "crack" — they must first break through the seed's tough protective coat. Clutching the seeds between their toes, jays hammer them open with their powerful beaks. Nuthatches also strike open seeds, but instead of holding them with their feet, they wedge the seeds under the bark of trees. Finch bills are used to open seeds in a much different fashion. Grosbeaks use their tongue to hold a seed in the furrows of the tough palate while, in a rapid forward and backward motion, the sharp edges of the beak remove the shell. Alternatively, the seed hull can be crushed by pressing it against the ridged, horny central surface of the upper mandible. With their vice-like bills, Evening Grosbeaks easily and noisily crush the stony pits of wild cherries.

American Tree Sparrows and other fine-billed seed-eaters select smaller seeds, often those of wildflowers. Even though their tools are more delicate, they are actually more efficient — up to three times faster — in handling and shelling small seeds than sparrows with heavier beaks, such as White-throated Sparrows. Some birds forgo the shelling until later. Quails and doves swallow small seeds intact and later deal with the tough items in their muscular stomach, the gizzard. The seeds are first stored in a special oesophageal pouch called the crop. This storage compartment allows birds to quickly gather a full meal and take it away to "eat" in a safe place — somewhat akin to bringing home a take-out meal from a fast-food restaurant. The seeds are released from the crop into the gizzard, where, along with grit and small stones also swallowed by the bird,

Great Crested Flycatchers (opposite) possess heavy beaks that deal quite nicely with dragonflies.
The inedible wings will be cut off and discarded before the meal is enjoyed.

they are thoroughly ground and crushed between the ridged, horny walls. The gizzard, much more developed in seed-eaters than in fruit-eaters, packs an impressive punch. The muscle-bound gizzard of a Wild Turkey can pulverize a pecan nut in less than an hour!

Besides a more developed gizzard, seed-eaters usually possess longer intestines than fruit-eaters and insectivores. In European Starlings, birds that dramatically shift their diet from animals in summer to plant material in winter, the intestine increases in length as the cold season approaches.

When prey becomes temporarily scarce, many insectivorous birds turn to plants for the energy necessary to carry them through the drought. On cold spring days I have seen birds as diverse as Blue-winged Warblers and Red-headed Woodpeckers feeding on Staghorn Sumach fruit. But some insectivores depend on plants for more than just a quick fix. An ability to digest the waxy coats of Bayberry fruit enables Yellow-rumped Warblers and Tree Swallows to spend winter months much farther north than others in their groups.

Fruit and seeds are not the only plant products that attract birds. Nectar is enjoyed by orioles and humming-birds, with the former often devouring the flowers in order to attain it. The long, thin bills (in some species adapted for specific shapes of flowers) and highly extensible tongues of hummingbirds can reach sugar-rich nectar in the deepest floral recess. Although the tongue is grooved and bifid, it does not act as a straw for sucking up the nectar. Instead, it absorbs nectar through capillary action; the sweet liquid is taken into the mouth with frequent licking motions.

Sap, not nectar, draws sapsuckers to plants. These unusual woodpeckers lap the sap that oozes from the distinctive neat rows of holes drilled into the trunks of birches, hemlocks, and other trees. The brush-like tip of their extensible tongue not only absorbs the sap but also picks up small insects that have come to feed, their bodies adorning the liquid like pieces of crackers floating in soup.

Nectar and sap, along with fruit and seeds, fail to satisfy all the nutritional needs of a bird. Protein and, to a lesser degree, fat must be acquired from other menus, the bodies of invertebrates being the most common source. Because these successful creatures can be found in every habitat, thriving equally well in coastal mud and forest canopies, they offer birds near-limitless feeding possibilities. And birds respond to this rich bounty in admirable fashion, with many species exploiting only certain groups of these abundant animals.

Beaks are the tools of choice for capturing small animal prey. Individually designed for extracting small creatures from nooks and crannies, bills take on every imaginable configuration. American Woodcocks sport Pinocchio-type beaks for probing the moist soil for earthworms. The highly sensitive tip can be opened and closed independent of the base. Brown Creepers have thin, curved bills, ideal for poking sideways under loose bark. The bills of woodpeckers are like chisels, stout and sharp for splintering wood and chipping bark. Thick skull bones and reinforced brains save these birds from knocking themselves silly as they drive their beaks into resistant wood.

With their fine bills, warblers and vireos, such as this Philadelphia Vireo (opposite top), glean small insects from their resting sites under leaves. In times of food stress, birds must become resourceful or perish. In a severe cold snap, when insects were hard to find, this male Scarlet Tanager (opposite bottom) found sustenance in the corpses of smelt strewn along a stony beach.

Woodpeckers use their beaks to access the food, but execute the capture with their highly extensible tongues. Glue-like saliva makes the barbed tongue particularly effective in wrenching insects from their maze of galleries in the wood.

Unlike woodpeckers, whose bills are similarly configured, the beaks of shorebirds vary tremendously and serve to capture specific prey. Plovers have short, stout bills for grabbing invertebrates that run across the sand. With their upturned bills, turnstones flip over rocks and other beach debris to reveal hidden treasures. Like little sewing machines, Dunlin rapidly probe the mud for shallowly buried worms and other tasty critters. Wading out into deeper water, godwits shove their formidable bills deep into the burrows of lugworms. And with a scythe-like motion, avocets sweep over the bottom, stirring insects and small crustaceans from their hiding places. This neat division of invertebrate resources makes it possible for a great mixture of shorebirds to forage together along the same stretch of shoreline.

Many different groups of birds feed on invertebrates. Ducks such as Northern Shovelers filter small aquatic animals from the water with their peculiar tongues and sieve-like bills. The aptly-named flycatchers sally forth from elevated perches and snatch insects out of the air. With their net-like gapes opened wide, nightjars, swallows, and swifts zoom through swarms of insects. Vireos and warblers roam the foliage, skillfully gleaning hidden treasures from leaves and twigs.

Although their foods often contain a fair amount of liquid, most birds (with the exception of hummingbirds) must regularly drink to replace water lost by breathing, flying, or excreting body wastes. Many dip their bills into water and tilt back their heads to let the liquid run down their throats. A few birds, including doves and fulmars, keep their bills submerged and suck up water. And when Northern Fulmars and other seabirds drink, they get more than just water, for seawater is about three percent salt. This level makes it impossible to rid their bodies of excess salt in the usual avian way, which is to release it in the urine. Instead, the salt is taken by the blood to large nasal glands above the eyes near the base of the bill. Here it is removed and ejected in almost twice its initial concentration. Some birds dribble the salty wastes out the beak; others out the nostrils. Albatrosses, petrels, fulmars, storm-petrels, and diving petrels are collectively known as "tubenoses" because their nostrils have been modified into paired tubes that are used for salt ejection as well as for breathing. Of this group, the petrels forcibly blow the wastes out of their tubed "noses" in a fashion resembling miniature canons going off.

To sustain their fervent activity, birds have developed an amazing variety of food preferences and feeding styles. But while invertebrates and plant products might be relatively easy to find and capture, a bird must consume a considerable amount to satisfy its needs. When the preferred course cannot be found in sufficient quantities or when it does not provide the full range of necessary nutrients, many birds compensate by switching foods either seasonally or as specific items become available. But not all birds dine on such bite-sized meals. Some find their sustenance in the bodies of much larger quarry.

CHAPTER FIVE

MERCHANTS OF DEATH

To observe a bird of prey make a kill is to witness nature at its savage finest: grace, power, and precision all melding into one brief moment of lethal magnificence. Unfortunately, we seldom look beyond that sudden moment of a life destroyed and fail to see the wonder of the biological process transpiring. Historically, man has not been kind to predatory birds, slaughtering countless thousands over the years. Attitudes have changed, fortunately, and most of our efforts today are dedicated to restoring, not obliterating, their populations.

"Eagle-eyed" aptly describes the eyesight of Golden Eagles (above) and other raptors, for their eyes act as miniature telescopes. Because of several modifications, the incoming image is enlarged about three times, allowing these magnificent birds to spot quarry over a mile (1.6 kilometers) away. American Kestrels (opposite) and all other birds of prey exhibit marvelous adaptations for locating and capturing prey. A kestrel's diet ranges from Meadow Voles (in this case) to small birds and insects. Other raptors are more specialized diners.

Predatory birds are finely-tuned killing machines, and each species in this diverse group is specialized for capturing certain types of prey. From elevated perches, American Kestrels swoop down and pounce on grasshoppers in sunny meadows. Bald Eagles slowly glide low over rivers, their massive feet suddenly snaring struggling salmon from the raging current. In full flight, Sharp-shinned Hawks acrobatically twist and turn, snatching Yellow-rumped Warblers right out of the air.

Food preferences vary between species, and possibly even within a predatory pair. In the accipiters, or bird hawks, the sexes differ quite remarkably in size, with females the larger of the two. While nesting energetics might be at play here, it is also possible that this dimorphism allows a male and female to exploit different sizes of prey in their territory. This would ensure a greater variety and number of quarry.

All avian hunters, regardless of their preferred cuisine, face daunting challenges inherent in a predatory lifestyle. A bird of prey must locate, capture, and kill its quarry before the rewards of the hunt are realized. For locating their prey, raptorial birds possess two acutely refined senses. The eyesight of hawks and eagles is highly developed, being two to three times more discriminating than ours. This acuity arises from an eye with an internal structure similar to that of a telescope. A large pupil and curved cornea let in plenty of light to provide a bright image. Because the lens is placed at some distance from the retina, by the time the incoming image reaches the back of the eye it is greatly enlarged. Light striking the retina excites countless cones; these sensory cells provide both visual acuity and color vision. The image is further enhanced in special retinal pits called foveae, which house as many as a million sensory cones. While many insectivorous birds have a single fovea in each eye, raptors and fish-eating birds, such as terns and kingfishers, possess two. It is believed that the central fovea may aid in the detection of prey and that the temporal fovea may play a key role during the pursuit. Regardless of how the foveae function, the image viewed by the raptor is bright, sharp, and enlarged.

Before it makes its final swoop or plunge, a raptor must be able to judge precisely the distance to its prey. Each eye affords a certain field of view; forward placement of the eyes creates a large overlap of the two fields, resulting in increased depth perception. Striated muscles enable the eyes to focus rapidly, thereby allowing the raptor to keep locked onto its target as it homes in on its mark, just like a guided missile.

Although hearing may play a secondary role to sight, it is also used to detect prey. The excited response elicited from a Northern Goshawk or Cooper's Hawk when one produces an injured rabbit sound by sucking on the back of the fingers is a testament to this. In raptors with developed hearing — Northern Harriers, for example — the muscular rim of the

Belted Kingfishers (opposite) also have enhanced vision for spotting underwater meals, such as this pet goldfish! Like hawks and terns, kingfishers possess two retinal pits packed with visual cells that provide unparalleled acuity.

An Osprey's diet consists exclusively of fish; they fearlessly plunge into water to grab their meals (opposite). A reversible toe and pointed scales on its feet (below) enable an Osprey to handle even the slipperiest fish with little problem.

external ear opening has been modified into a funnel for gathering sound. Not surprisingly, Ospreys, to whom hearing is of no use in finding their underwater quarry, have no funnel at all.

Owls, like their diurnal counterparts, the hawks, also locate prey by sight and sound. But because they have mastered the night, a time that offers unique challenges, owls possess a number of novel adaptations. Their eyes, located on the front of their dish-shaped faces, have large corneas; when dilated, the large pupils collect what little light there is. Unlike that of a diurnal raptor, an owl's lens is quite round and is placed much closer to the retina, which is also highly curved. The result of this odd configuration is a tubular-shaped eye, one that allows for image enlargement without much loss of light. As light passes through the lens onto the curved retina, it is spread out, and the incoming image is magnified. The brightness results from

light travelling a shorter distance from the lens to the retina than in the eye of a diurnal raptor. Light striking the retina excites the densely packed sensory cells, which consist mainly of rods, not cones. Although rods may not provide the visual acuity of cones, they are far more sensitive to lower levels of light and thus better serve the needs of these hunters of the dark.

Even though their frontally-placed eyes provide binocular vision, many owls improve their perception of distance by rapidly bobbing their heads in a circular fashion. This comical movement provides an owl with different perspectives on an object of interest, allowing it to determine its location more precisely.

In a world of darkness, however, sight pales in importance to hearing. An owl's auditory senses have been honed to unparalleled levels, with a few — Barn Owls included — able to

Gangs of Harris' Hawks (below) cooperate not only in hunting but also in their breeding efforts. When fishing, Tricolored Herons may hold a wing or two over the water in a posture called mantling (opposite). The shadow cast by the wing may lure fish into a false sense of security; it may also reduce glare off the water, allowing the heron to better see into the water.

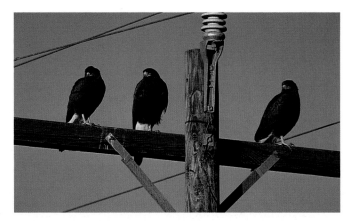

locate and capture prey by hearing alone. Sounds are picked up by the ear openings, large slots on the sides of the wide skull. Because of the skull's width, a sound arrives at each opening at a slightly different time. A mere 0.000,03 second difference is enough for an owl to get a directional fix on a rustling mouse. To further enhance the owl's ability to pinpoint its target, the ear openings are asymmetrically shaped and offset. On the leading edge of the ear openings, movable skin flaps capture and direct sound coming from behind the bird.

The "wise" appearance for which owls are famous — a round, flat face bearing large eyes — may well assist in hearing. The dish-like shape catches sound, which the concentric rings of hardened feather edges direct to the ear openings. Interestingly, Northern Harriers, which hunt by ear in the day, have a similar facial configuration.

Once prey is located, it must be captured. Most fish-eating birds, such as loons, cormorants, herons, and king-

fishers, use their beaks to capture the prey. Many of these use their tongue to help secure the meal once it is inside the bill. Loggerhead and Northern Shrikes use their massive beaks to capture prey by pummelling their victims into submission. Raptors, though, rarely use their bills; rather, their strong feet equipped with massive talons are usually the tools of choice.

While most diurnal raptors have three toes forward and one back, Ospreys are unique in having two back. But as the outer back toe of these expert fishermen is reversible, it can be directed forward as well. This flexibility, also found in owls, may help these birds capture their prey under less than ideal conditions: underwater for Ospreys and in darkness for owls. To aid their fishing efforts, Ospreys also have another unusual adaptation. Prickly scales on the soles of their feet provide a better grip for slippery meals.

Raptors demonstrate great ingenuity in capturing their prey. Red-tailed Hawks, Broad-winged Hawks, and many other

Great Gray Owls (opposite) hunt in the day as well as at night. Unlike most other birds of prey, these and other owls depend on slow, silent flight for capturing prey, and the leading edge of their wings has a special fringe that provides them with the necessary stealth (below).

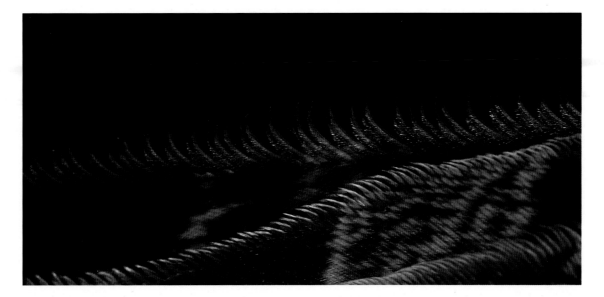

buteos patiently sit in ambush until a meal appears, then quickly drop onto it. With speeds exceeding 150 miles (250 kilometers) an hour, a Peregrine Falcon dives down (stoops) from great heights onto its victim, striking and raking it with open talons in an explosion of feathers. A Sharp-shinned Hawk streaks into a flock of songbirds, singles out an individual, and doggedly pursues it into dense shrubbery.

While most raptors hunt alone, there is one that often hunts in the company of others. In the scorching southwestern desert, a gang of Harris' Hawks takes turns flushing a Desert Cottontail from cactus patches until the terrified creature makes a fatal mistake. Hunting cooperatively makes it possible to capture elusive animals, prey that a lone Harris'

Hawk would be hard-pressed to catch. While food capture seems to be the obvious reason for this association, there may actually be genetic reasons behind the cooperative efforts. Members of a group may be related and breed cooperatively, with several males helping out with the nest duties, or smaller groups might consist of a female with not one but two mates.

Hawks on the hunt display other surprising behaviors. I have watched a Northern Harrier repeatedly pluck Meadow Vole nests from the ground, then fly up about 20 feet (7 meters) above the ground before dropping them. After hovering for a couple of seconds, the harrier dove to the ground and gobbled up the apparently dazed voles as they staggered out of the broken nest.

Here's blinking at you! A "third eyelid," the nictitating membrane cleanses and moisturizes a bird's eye. In most birds it is drawn across the eye from the inner corner outward so rapidly that it cannot be seen; but in owls, including this Great Horned Owl (opposite), it is often drawn slowly and can be easily viewed. During capture of its prey, an owl's upper eyelids close to protect the eyes.

Bills have been modified in many ways for capturing fish. Great Egrets grab small fish with the tips of their bills (top left), Anhingas spear their prey (top right), and mergansers, including this Hooded Merganser (above left), grasp the slippery creatures with their serrated bills, well developed in this female Common Merganser (above right).

Sharp-shinned Hawks (above left) and other raptors are interested only in the nutrient-rich flesh, not the bones or feathers. They pluck their prey, such as this European Starling, before gleaning the flesh from the bones. When a hawk is finished feeding, little is left of its victim, including this House Sparrow (above right).

Predators often swallow small prey whole, later regurgitating the inedible parts in a pellet. Pellets such as this Barred Owl offering (below left) contain valuable information about the small mammals living in the owl's area (below right).

Speed and surprise are a diurnal hunter's two main weapons. But if owls were to fly with raptor wings, they would go very hungry indeed. Fast flight requires stiff, strong feathers that inevitably produce a whistling noise as air moves over them (just as do the wings of an airplane). In the silence of the night, such an obvious sound would soon warn any small rodent. To gain a necessary advantage over their prey, owls have sacrificed speed for silence. A comb-like projection on the leading flight feathers breaks the air and eliminates the noisy turbulence as the wing slices through the darkness. Most other feathers have loose, soft edges, and the wings are huge in relation to the light weight they bear. All these features provide owls with the deadly stealth needed to surprise their ever-alert prey.

Once captured, an animal must be dispensed with quickly, as flailing claws and sharp teeth can inflict serious injury. Accipiters squeeze their prizes, their needle-sharp talons piercing vital internal organs. Golden Eagles strike larger prey with their massive beaks, while owls snap necks with theirs. Dense feathers on the body or legs absorb most of a prey's futile attempts to escape, and the eyes are protected by the closure of an eyelid (in owls it is the upper) during the fatal strike.

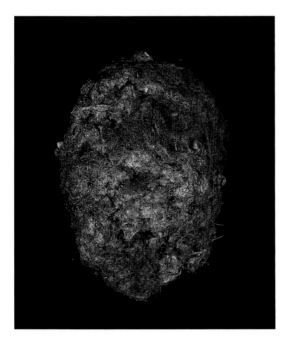

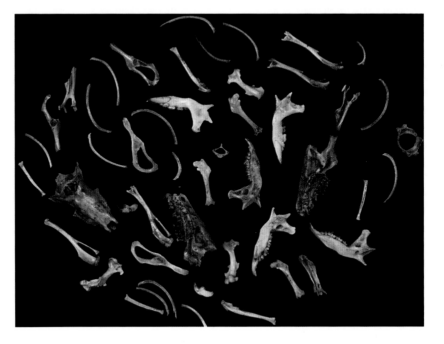

Although animal flesh is considerably easier to digest than tough plant tissue, other parts of the meal are quite indigestible. Fur, feathers, scales, shells, bones, teeth, nails, and even the outer skeletons of insects are hard to break down and offer little nutrition. If the prey is large enough, the predator eats the "good stuff" and leaves the rest. Accipiters and falcons pick the flesh off the bones after first plucking the feathers from their meal to get at the meat.

But smaller meals are hardly worth the effort, and so shrews, mice, voles, and other small prey are often swallowed whole. Internally, raptorial birds have evolved a neat way of dealing with the undesired portions of their meals. The first stomach is glandular and douses the food in enzymes. The next stomach, the gizzard, holds back the inedible portions while the liquified meal gets passed on for further absorption. Now neatly rolled into an oblong pellet, the unwanted material gets moved back into the glandular part of the stomach, from where it is eventually coughed up and expelled. While owls and hawks are best known for this feature, numerous other birds, including grebes, herons, and ravens, also form pellets.

Most predators are not above dining on a carcass, particularly in times of stress. For a few, such as Golden and Bald Eagles, scavenging contributes greatly to their winter survival. Gulls and vultures eagerly seek out cadavers at all times, regardless of how putrid the meal might be. Vultures are particularly adapted for harvesting a living from the dead. Featherless heads facilitate reaching into rotting corpses with little contamination of plumage. Turkey Vultures can even locate a carcass by smell, an ability that Black Vultures, their olfactory-challenged cousins, may exploit by following them on foraging expeditions. Turkey Vultures will also follow each other to a carcass, which may be one reason these specialized birds roost in large congregations.

The life of a bird of prey is not an easy one. Its daily quest for food is fraught with effort and risk. And, just like fruit- and insect-eaters, predatory birds are slave to the fluctuations of their food supply: when prey is abundant, they thrive; when prey is scarce, they starve or strike out blindly in search of richer hunting grounds. For those that move on, the journey may prove arduous and unrewarding. In times of famine, even the greatest of hunters may fall victim to an unkind fate.

A putrid corpse can be a messy meal, so a lack of head feathers can be of benefit, particularly when the head is shoved right into the corpse, as Black Vultures (opposite left) and their relatives do. A predatory lifestyle is fraught with hardship, including injury incurred during the chase. This Sharp-shinned Hawk (opposite right) was impaled by a pruned branch during its last aggressive chase.

CHAPTER SIX

THE
JOURNEY

As summer wanes in temperate regions, vanishing acts are performed all through the land. Flying insects quietly exit, most leaving behind a legacy of eggs and larvae stuffed into hidden recesses. Reptiles and amphibians retire into the bowels of the earth, not to appear again until the spring sun has broken winter's spell. The snows of late autumn blanket seeds and small mammals, placing them beyond the reach of most of their feathered foes. As feast fades into famine, birds must adapt or perish.

In winter, short-term food caches are made by a few birds of prey. Northern Shrikes often stash mice and voles (above, a White-footed Mouse) in the forks of small trees. Migrating birds (opposite) use a number of guidance systems to find their way, including the earth's magnetic field, the sun, stars, even the moon.

Some prepare for the lean times by storing food when it is plentiful. Several members of the corvid family are particularly noted for caching. In cool northern forests and bogs, Gray Jays ceaselessly store food all summer and fall, each small parcel carefully wrapped in a salival pall. The sticky saliva bonds the package under bark or lichen, holding it there for much later dining. Whether because of its special coating or chemicals present in its resting site (or both), the food remains edible throughout the warm months preceding winter's deep freeze, and in total may persist as long as three-quarters of a year. Clark's Nutcrackers do not coat their food with protective spit, but the seeds they prefer have tough coats that provide ample protection against the elements. These raucous birds hoard seeds in numerous small stashes as far away as 13 miles (22 kilometers) from the source tree. A need to compensate for theft by squirrels and other seed-eaters, not greed, drives a nutcracker to store far more seeds than it can possibly eat in the coming winter and spring. A single bird may hide as many as 30,000 seeds, creating a sizable surplus that benefits not only other animals but the pines themselves, since some seeds will survive and bring forth new trees.

Gray Jays and Clark's Nutcrackers create food caches all through their territory (a behavior called scatter hoarding), and then rely on an incredible spatial memory and familiarity with their domain to relocate them later. Acorn Woodpeckers, on the other hand, generally maintain only one or two central hoards, known as granaries. A single tree can house up to 50,000 acorns, each tightly jammed into a hole. Created by a group effort, the granaries are closely guarded against thieves.

Few birds, however, expend this much energy in creating food stores. Black-capped Chickadees and a few birds of prey, among others, make small, short-term caches. Chickadee stores provide a quick fix of energy-rich food, which is extremely important in surviving a cold winter snap. When hunting is good, some predators cache their untouched bounty, returning to it when needed. Shrikes leave their surplus prey impaled on a sharp object (such as a thorn) or draped over a fork in a branch. Owls often lodge their uneaten food in coniferous boughs where, in winter, it remains nicely refrigerated. Before devouring a frozen meal, several species, including Northern Saw-whet and Great Horned Owls, thaw it first by sitting on it.

Birds that hoard benefit by having reserves to hold them over during a tough period (which, for some birds, may last months). But if all the food should be depleted, a bird's fate may well be sealed. Most birds never take this risk, and so when their summer food supply begins to dry up, they abandon ship and head for richer pastures (or forests or waters).

By the time the Tamaracks flame gold, not all birds have fled northern haunts. Gray Jays (opposite) remain to challenge the oncoming winter. By creating thousands of small caches all through their territories, these gentle birds find sufficient food to see them through the tough boreal winter.

Acorn Woodpeckers (below) create huge communal stores of acorns, which are aggressively defended by the group that stashes them. To reach their wintering grounds, migrating birds (opposite) traverse great distances, passing through or over terrain dramatically different than that found in their summer haunts.

Black-and-white Warblers (below) and other small birds often double their body weight by building up large deposits of fat to be used as fuel during their great journeys. Arctic Terns (opposite top) have been aptly deemed the champions of migration, for their round trips can span an incredible 12,500 miles (20,000 kilometers). Large birds, including Turkey Vultures (opposite bottom), employ an energy-efficient gliding flight during migration.

Sometimes the move is relatively short, only half a province or state away. Northern finches, for example, closely follow the regional crops of birches and conifers. When bumper seed crops appear in an area, it is not long until hordes, or "irruptions," of these gypsy birds arrive. The biology of crossbills is closely linked to their food supply. When they encounter a particularly rich crop of seeds, they often stay and nest, regardless of the season. As a result, these nomadic birds have been known to produce eggs even in the dead of winter.

For most birds, however, the journey at summer's end is anything but short. Insectivorous birds breeding in temperate regions often winter in tropical lands, traversing thousands of miles between their two homes. Townsend's Warblers leave the cool northwestern Pacific slopes in favor of the misty Central American mountains. Scarlet Tanagers trade the maple woods of the northeast for Brazilian rainforests. Yet, the distances flown

to these winter retreats, while impressive, pale in comparison to the travels undertaken by the undisputed champion of migration, the Arctic Tern. Without the aid of tune-ups and with feathers the only parts replaced, many of these hardy terns fly from the eastern Arctic to the Antarctic via Africa, an astounding 12,500 miles (20,000 kilometers) round trip. Just think of the frequent flier points these worldly wanderers might accumulate in their ten-year life!

Ample food and hospitable climates are migration's rewards. But the journeys are not without cost or risk. Vast amounts of fuel and finely-tuned navigational systems are mandatory equipment for these lengthy excursions, and there is greater exposure to predators, inclement weather, and man-made hazards, such as towers and power lines. No small wonder that only about half the birds attempting such a journey make it back successfully each year.

WILD WINGS

*Semipalmated Sandpipers (opposite) and other migrating birds require stopover sites for refueling
and rest during their lengthy journeys.*

As summer passes, the shortening of the days triggers a flurry of feeding activity. Stores of fat, the only source of fuel for the upcoming trip, quickly accumulate under the skin, in muscles, and around the wishbone, liver, and gut. By the time they begin their sojourn, small birds such as Blackpoll Warblers have doubled their body weight. The excess weight never lasts long, however. As a bird steadily wings its way along the chosen route, the fat is burned and the bird grows lighter. With a lesser load to move, the bird's fuel efficiency increases, with an ounce (28 grams) of fat near the end of the journey yielding two and a half times its initial output.

Every effort is made to stretch vital energy reserves during migration. Even flight becomes more energy-efficient. Small birds typically use an aerodynamic "bounding," a roller-coaster flight consisting of bursts of rapid flapping alternated with periods of closed-wing gliding. Raptors and other large birds such as gulls also conserve energy by gliding, but with their wings stiffly braced open, not closed. A highly-efficient form of flight, soaring uses only about a twentieth of the energy burned by flapping. Whenever possible, the energy spent by flapping to regain altitude is saved by soaring on rising thermals of air. Because birds can cover great distances on very little energy by riding thermals, many hawks time their migration to maximize their use of these elevators of air. Few avian spectacles are more spectacular than the annual fall movement of Broad-winged Hawks along the north shore of Lake Erie. Countless thousands merge into a swirling, living current that slowly, methodically drifts southwestward across the autumn sky.

Along the way, long-distance migrants make periodic pit stops to refuel and recharge. Thrushes, warblers, and other songbirds usually put down after flying several hundred miles. Shorebirds stop less frequently, traversing as much as 2,500 miles (4,000 kilometers) between stopovers. After refuelling in the Bay of Fundy — where they double their body weight in ten days — Arctic-nesting Semipalmated Sandpipers fly non-stop, for three and a half days, to Suriname, South America.

As an excessive amount of heat is generated during flight, many migrating birds travel at high altitudes where temperatures are lower. Here, the birds are air-cooled and water normally lost to evaporative cooling is conserved. Shorebirds occasionally migrate higher than three and a half miles (6 kilometers) above the ground, while small birds generally fly at heights about a quarter of that.

In addition to a reduced risk of dehydration, there is usually less wind at higher altitudes. For the migrating bird, this is an important factor; for while tail-winds might be favorable for migration, cross-winds and strong head-winds drain a bird's energy. Under calm conditions, a Ruby-throated Hummingbird's fuel reserves would carry it almost 1,400 miles (2,300 kilometers); against even light head-winds, the same bird would run out of fuel after covering less than half that distance.

Exactly how a bird is able to leave its breeding grounds, travel thousands of miles to foreign lands, and return to the same location the following year is still largely a mystery. Obviously, some sort of guidance system must be in place. In fact, research has revealed that birds use a number of

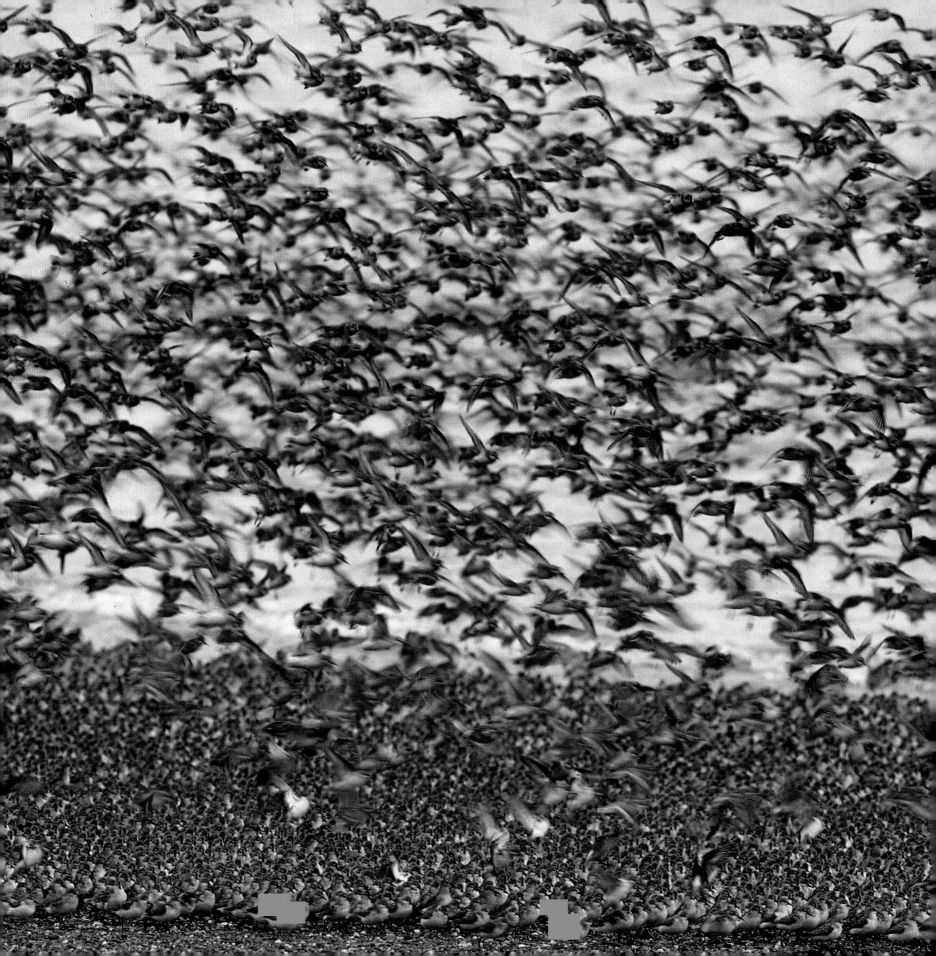

Indigo Buntings (below) have been used in studies that confirm the use of star constellations as guidance aids.
One of the greatest of all natural history phenomena, migration (opposite) is also one of the most poorly understood.

environmental compasses. Night-migrating birds such as Indigo Buntings use stellar constellations as a visual road map. And many night fliers take off at sunset, perhaps using the sunset point or sky polarization as orientation cues for the beginning of their journey. For those birds that fly during the day — hawks, swallows, hummingbirds, and Blue Jays, for example — the sun and visible landforms undoubtedly serve as navigational aids. The earth's magnetic field also plays some role in navigation. It was originally thought that this field could be detected by anomalous particles of magnetite embedded in a bird's head; researchers now believe that the field interacts with photopigments in the eye. The magnetic field is probably used in conjunction with other orientation systems, and may even serve as an auxiliary system when others become disabled, such as when cloud cover obscures the sun.

A number of other compasses may well exist. The moon, infrasound (far-carrying sound, such as the surf crashing or wind howling across mountains), and specific smells emitted by the land or sea have all been offered as possible sources of navigational information for birds. Perhaps learning even plays a role, as it might for young Canada Geese, which tag along with their parents on the first family trip south.

Of all natural history phenomena, migration remains one of the greatest and most enigmatic. Although the costs of migration may seem excessive, they are probably no greater than those inherent in other solutions to winter. In Nature, several truths prevail. All living things deal with challenges, and while each is resolved in a great many ways, every solution involves hidden costs. No living thing, feathered or otherwise, is ever given a free ride in life.

CHAPTER SEVEN

LOVE, LUST, AND BROKEN PROMISES

As the warmth of spring embraces the land, countless plants and animals are gently liberated from their winter-long quiescence. The first trickle of life gradually becomes a rising flood, flowing northward with dramatic speed. Following closely in the wake of this rejuvenation, long-absent birds return to their old haunts, joining those species that stayed to weather winter's hardships. Migrants and residents alike restlessly search for more than just the bounty that the awakening land offers. With ardor and determination, they go about the serious business of finding a mate.

The song of a male Eastern Meadowlark (above) contains important clues as to his suitability as a mate. This female House Finch (opposite) is probably unimpressed by what she sees, for females of her species prefer males sporting only the finest plumage. She would do better by a male with more intense color, since this trait reflects a superior ability to forage, an important consideration for a female who is mate-shopping.

For Marsh Wrens (below), the size of a male's song repertoire, as well as the number of dummy nests he can offer as gifts,
may provide a female with essential information about her main concern — the quality of his territory. Mating is as complicated
as it is fascinating. Before a pair ends up conjugating their relationship — as these Greater Roadrunners are doing (opposite) — a complex
volley of offerings and rejections, signals and counter-signals usually transpire.

All living things are driven to reproduce, and birds are no exception. Producing offspring allows a bird to perpetuate part of its unique genetic makeup. And if its progeny and their descendants continue to pass on their genetic inheritance, immortality of a sort can be achieved. With such high stakes, finding a mate in the breeding season assumes even greater importance.

The drive to find a mate transforms even the meek into theatrical showpieces and the mute into melodious songsters. The males most often don the nuptial apparel and vigorously vie for the favors of the opposite sex. Females are usually loathe to give themselves to just any male that comes along. As their investment of resources into the production of young exceeds that of their partners, it is more prudent for a female to choose a mate who is a good provider and defender or, at the very least, who will contribute good genetic material.

A female encounters many males during the breeding season, all proclaiming their worth. To make a wise choice, she has to peer through the veil of sweet offerings and determine whether a suitor is all he claims to be. This task is made somewhat easier if a male's stature is manifested in a prominent physical attribute or outlandish act. A female uses such a feature as a yardstick for measuring a male's relative worth. Numerous studies of both wild and captive birds have confirmed that males with an exceptional feature are often met with open wings (and raised tail), while those less richly-endowed get rebuffed. Female-generated discrimination, part of a powerful force called sexual selection, has led to the refinement and proliferation of many magnificent predominately-male traits, including brilliant colors, elaborate ornaments, intricate displays, and vibrant songs.

Through song, a male expresses desire and intent without expending vast amounts of energy. Each bird's song is a species-specific coat of arms, but subtle variations in duration, pitch, phrase, and size of repertoire combine to make each singer's offering a distinctive calling card. This uniqueness also provides for female discrimination.

Certain elements in a male's song may hold particular appeal to the listener. In some species, such as Swamp Sparrows and Red-winged Blackbirds, males with the most extensive song repertoire draw the strongest responses from females. A female's interest may also be piqued by the amount of song. Singing requires time, and so a male who spends a lot of time serenading could well be occupying a territory with a wealth of easily accessed food.

Although each species owns a unique vocal nametag, variations of a single theme song occur in many species. A Canyon Wren has three different versions in its repertoire, while a Marsh Wren might offer more than a hundred distinct scores. But few species come close to matching the number of ditties sung by a Brown Thrasher; over a thousand renditions are included in its song sheets. Whether large or small, repertoire size can offer distinct advantages to a songbird. Birds with small repertoires — White-throated Sparrows have only one song type — can easily learn their neighbors' songs. When it recognizes the song as not belonging to a stranger, a territorial male saves the energy that would normally be spent on an aggressive reaction — unless the neighbor becomes overly friendly and crosses their mutual property line!

Common Snipes (above) announce territories and sexual desires by "winnowing" over their domains. Modified outer tail feathers produce the peculiar hollow "laughter" that reverberates over wetlands.

The striking difference in appearances between male (below left) and female (below right) birds is epitomized in these Vermilion Flycatchers. This exaggerated feature results from female choice.

An Atlantic Puffin's sexual maturity is indicated through its bill structure. Males gradually acquire grooves in the red portion, taking four years to develop just two grooves. These young males (above left) that are sorting out their differences lack bill grooves, so would be ignored by any respectable female. The older individual (above right), however, would likely be considered by any female to be quite groovy!

Since females are often courted by a number of desiring males, they can afford to be choosy.
Below, a female Ring-necked Duck is presented with a lot of choice!

Producing a song that is hard to learn also has its advantages. Greater complexity may make it difficult for a neighbor to memorize the full repertoire and recognize the singer. Thinking that the songster is a stranger and therefore a potential intruder, the neighbor might spend more time and effort on boundary surveillance. This increase in vigilance could interfere with his efforts in attracting a mate, all to the benefit of the innately devious singer, who just keeps on singing.

The size and nature of the song repertoire may differ with the type of breeding system. White-throated Sparrows, Canyon Wrens, and most warblers, birds with small song repertoires, are usually monogamous, and the males offer extensive care for the young. Their songs are generally quite musical, dominated by whistles and pure tones. Marsh Wrens and Red-winged Blackbirds, which have extensive repertoires, are polygynous breeders; a male usually mates with a number of females. Since the males offer little assistance in the rearing of

young, perhaps they need to compete for females more vigorously through song. As a rule, polygynous birds (Yellow-headed Blackbirds being a notable example) produce song that is loud and dominated by low-pitched buzzes, clicks, and slurs, a quality that has been referred to as being "pugilistic." Whether or not this type of song reflects the singer's disposition, quality territories are certainly worth fighting for, and males holding exceptionally good territories usually attract the most mates. While territory quality might be reflected in food abundance, for Dickcissels and Lark Buntings it is the availability of appropriate nest sites that determines the number of females that settle in a male's territory.

The relationship between repertoire size and mating system does not always hold true. The monogamous breeding strategies of Northern Mockingbirds and Brown Thrashers does not explain their vast song repertoires. Undoubtedly, other factors, such as the nature of the habitat, are also important influences.

As females often prefer mature, experienced males for mates, some males announce their sexual maturity with badges of status. Cedar Waxwing males (opposite, top left) usually do not acquire their red ornamentation until they are two years old. Badges of maturity and superiority can also be directed towards other males. The brilliant epaulettes of male Red-winged Blackbirds (opposite, top right) are covered when not needed for territorial announcements.

Certain song types may communicate different messages to different audiences. Many warblers, including Ovenbirds, Yellow Warblers, and Black-and-white Warblers, produce two types of song, one more common at the start of the breeding period and the other more frequent either late in that season or during interactions with other males. While the early song may serve a dual purpose in advertising sexual availability and territorial ownership, the later song may play more of a role in announcing property rights. Also, during the breeding season many thrushes and warblers sing in the dark of the pre-dawn and late in the evening. Quite possibly these before-and-after-hours songs serve more as "no trespassing" warnings to other males than as "good morning" or "good night" tributes to their mates!

A bird that lacks a refined voice is not prevented from audibly communicating its desire or territory ownership. High over wetlands, a Common Snipe's stiff outer-tail feathers vibrate wildly during a dive, producing the peculiar winnowing sound that resembles more a maniacal laugh than a bird noise. As a male Spruce Grouse struts before a scrutinizing female, his tail feathers noisily swish open and closed. His wings also announce his presence, with noisy flutter flights punctuating the performance. As they spiral up into the dusk sky, American Woodcocks whistle short bursts of tunes with their slotted outer three primaries. And wings produce both the loud claps heralding the nuptial flights of Short- and Long-eared Owls and the thunderous drumming that permeates spring woods. Perched atop a moss-covered log, a Ruffed Grouse rapidly pounds his wings forward and upward against the air to announce his presence. Drumming of a different nature rattles from high overhead in the forest. By striking their beaks rapidly against dead wood (or, in some cases, metal), both male and female woodpeckers hammer out a resonating drum roll that, like song, attracts mates and defines territories.

In the avian world, appearances are important: the dazzling colors and conspicuous patterns that dominate spring plumages are, for the most part, designed to win the eye of discriminating females. Many female birds do, in fact, choose the best-

Male Common Goldeneyes perform highly ritualized head movements to attract a female's attention (opposite, bottom left). A female may gain better feeding sites and reduced harassment by other males if she stays near a dominant male. A chosen male will not be rewarded for several months, however, because the female will only mate when she returns to her breeding grounds. Both sexes of Black Terns take part in feeding the young (opposite, bottom right). By also presenting the females with gifts of food during courtship, the males offer them a chance to evaluate their worth as fathers.

*The elaborate displays of a male Spruce Grouse (opposite) amplify the magnificence of his plumage
as he attempts to impress a potential mate.*

dressed beaus. Male Mallards in their fullest breeding plumage are preferred to those clothed only in partial garb, and the most vividly colored male House Finches are the first to be given the nod of approval. Since bright color can reflect maturity, vitality, dominance, or, as in the case of House Finches, a superior foraging ability, choosing a vividly plumaged male can result in the successful rearing of healthy young.

Color can also communicate messages between members of the same sex. The brilliant red epaulettes of male Red-winged Blackbirds not only impress females but, perhaps more importantly, intimidate inferior males. Because these badges inspire as well as infer aggression, they are usually concealed until needed. Avoiding peer aggression may well be the reason that the yearling males of some species possess female-like or partial male plumage (a phenomenon known as delayed plumage maturation) during the breeding season. While female choice underlies much of the richness in male color and song, competition between males is also an important influence.

Ornamental plumes and other specific features of a potential mate's attire may catch the eye of a discerning female. A particularly prominent endowment may indicate superiority, for the male can still feed, and survive, despite such an obvious handicap. A conspicuous feature may also be a sign of exceptional health or superior genes. Whatever the underlying message, many females choose mates on the basis of their appearance. In Barn Swallow circles, the bigger the better appears to be the thinking, for females generally prefer males with the longest tails. There is evidence, in fact, that tails do "say something"

about their bearer. Studies conducted on Barn Swallows in Scandinavia have uncovered an amazing relationship between tail length and resistance to parasites. It's safe to assume, therefore, that when females select a male bearing a particularly splendid feature, they are very likely receiving benefits with far greater significance than simple visual gratification.

In a male's efforts to win over a female, however, it may not only be what he has but how he uses it that determines his success. Bold patterns and ornate feathers become even more arresting when woven into the fabric of elegant presentation. Ritualized movements of the head, wings, and tail can accentuate specific sexual signals, providing yet another mechanism for discrimination by females. Male Hooded Mergansers raise and lower dramatic black-bordered white crests, rendered even more obvious by a sideways shaking of the head. A Great Blue Heron's neck plumes, along with a bright bill and chestnut wing linings, are showcased during the bird's elaborate stretch display.

Although they consume more energy, visual displays are similar to songs in that they can also be directed to other males, as well as offered in concert with other forms of advertisement. Females do, in fact, select males on the basis of their performances. Over grassy meadows, male Bobolinks perform courtship song-flights. While delivering their peculiar song (somewhat reminiscent of the sound of that annoying robot in *Star Wars*), they flutter over fields on stiff, downturned wings. The preferred mates are those that give the longest displays, as a female who is paired with a superior performer is more successful in raising young.

Communal displays are held by promiscuous species, such as Wild Turkeys (opposite). Females carefully watch the males strut their stuff. A particularly impressive male usually ends up with more than his fair share of matings — unfair at least in the eyes of the majority of males who usually fail to mate.

Since displays can convey different messages to different audiences, a species might use a wide variety in its courtship and territorial communications. By mixing and matching any number of the 16 displays in its repertoire, a Great Egret can deliver a highly personalized message to its onlooker.

In species where the males "love them and leave them," courtship antics can reach the spectacular. Particularly impressive are the communal displays of Sage Grouse, Sharp-tailed Grouse, and Lesser and Greater Prairie-Chickens. Each spring, the males gather in courtship arenas known as leks, where they sort out individual display sites, with dominant males occupying the most central territories. In an incredible pageantry of song, dance, and color, the males strive to win the attention of the females, who, like judges at a talent show, carefully evaluate the performances. Competition is intense, but the rewards are great — the winner's prize being a promiscuous binge. Those few who end up fertilizing most of the females are chosen on a variety of criteria ranging from the intensity of their dance to the color and condition of their inflated neck sacs. Any male Sage Grouse whose yellow sacs sport the telltale blemishes of lice occupancy seldom gets "lekky" in these tournaments of love.

In polygynous and lekking species, males do the courting and females assume most of the parental responsibilities after mating. But these roles are reversed in a few species. In Spotted Sandpipers, Wilson's Phalaropes, Red Phalaropes, and Red-necked Phalaropes, it is the females who are larger, more colorful (at least in the phalaropes), and actively compete for mates. Once a male in any of these species accepts the proposition of a lustful female, he is promptly saddled with a clutch of eggs and she heads off in search of yet another willing peon. In these polyandrous shorebirds, several males may end up each incubating a separate clutch while the female tends to other business. In some groups of Harris' Hawks, polyandry also prevails, but unlike the sequential mating that occurs in liberated shorebirds, the female hawk mates with several males at the same time. The entire group shares in more than just carnal pleasure, however, for they all participate in rearing the ensuing batch of mixed-parentage young.

Bigamy, promiscuity, and group sex — these matrimonial predilections might make birds seem a rather lascivious lot. In reality, though, these behaviors are in the minority, with most birds exchanging the vows of monogamy. One of the main benefits of monogamy over most other breeding strategies is that the offspring usually receive extensive biparental care.

The bonds formed between monogamous pairs rarely last beyond one breeding season; a few birds may even change partners between successive nestings in the same season. Usually only the larger (and longer-lived) species bond for several years, with geese, swans, and eagles among the very few that exchange the vow "until death do we part."

Monogamy might seem a somewhat more "morally correct" strategy, but it does not prevent a bird from playing the field. Paternity studies have revealed that many monogamous birds sneak extra-pair copulations when their partner's back is turned, resulting in mixed-paternity broods. More than a third of the young of Purple Martins, Indigo Buntings, and Bobolinks might

Appearances and roles are reversed in Wilson's Phalaropes (below), where the brightly-colored females court the males.
These liberated birds select not one but several males to father successive clutches of their eggs. Mated pairs, such as Northern Gannets (opposite),
would be wise to keep an eye on each other, for many birds are not above "playing the field" in order to produce superior young.

be fathered outside of mated pairs. In some cases, a male might even end up caring for an entire brood that he had no hand in producing! To a participating male, the advantages of extra-pair copulations are clear: he sires more offspring carrying his genes. But a female can also benefit from an adulterous foray if her inseminator is of a higher quality than her mate. A female's decision to sneak in a quick neighborly visit might easily be made on a sight-unseen basis, with the quality of the neighbor's song supplying her with enough incentive.

Because the risk of cuckoldry is real, males take great pains to guarantee the paternity of their offspring. Territorial boundaries are enthusiastically defended, and males stay close to their mates, becoming intrepid bodyguards during the critical pre-laying and egg-laying periods. Frequent copulations, especially after the appearance of an intruder, flood the female's repro-

ductive tract with sperm, helping the male ensure his claim to paternity. Even if a stranger did sneak in a copulation, the large amount of the territorial male's sperm would likely swamp the stranger's, lessening its chances of successfully fertilizing an egg. From the male's perspective, this might well be considered, as so aptly put by one author, "making the best of a bad situation!"

Variety is indeed the spice of life when it comes to the sexual escapades of birds. However perplexing the great diversity of breeding strategies might seem, each must necessarily offer a certain degree of success in order to persist, with success being measured by the passage of genes into the next generation. But a bird's efforts to perpetuate its identity are seldom finished with the production of eggs. For not until the young have reached a certain level of independence is the task anywhere near complete.

Chapter Eight

FUTURE RETURNS AND THE ECONOMICS OF LIFE

Once the curtains have been drawn on the melodrama of courtship, far less glamorous roles await the triumphant players. In the encore performance, tedious labor replaces passionate revelry as parenthood takes the stage. Most birds play the part of parent with gusto, investing considerable time and energy into the care of eggs and young. Raising a brood, however, lessens a bird's chances of surviving and successfully producing future offspring. To maximize the return of its parental investment, a bird must innately weigh the costs of its current reproductive effort against the dividends realized not only from this endeavor but from all future ones, as well. A bird that invests wisely is rewarded with a piece of the future; one that wagers poorly stands to lose all.

Genes are the currency of life, and a bird's young, such as these Barn Swallows (above), are their couriers. Killdeers and many other ground-nesting birds often lay their eggs in little more than a shallow scrape (opposite).

Even though Ovenbirds nest on the ground, they still make a developed nest (opposite left) because it must shelter not only the eggs but also the nestlings once they hatch. Usually, only larger birds such as Great Blue Herons use their same nests for a number of successive years (opposite right).

The number of eggs laid by a bird can never be used as a measure of its reproductive success, for the odds are poor that any given egg will develop into an adult bird. Predation, abandonment, infertility, and environmental unkindness — the deck is clearly stacked against an embryo. Even after hatching, many nestlings fall victim to the harsh reality of the natural world. Only when its young are completely independent does a bird have even a reasonable chance of reaping any reward for its efforts.

Despite holding the key to a bird's genetic future, eggs are seldom treated like gold. Many ground-nesting birds, such as Killdeers, Black Skimmers, and Least Terns, put little effort into nest-building apart from digging a modest shallow scrape in which they lay their eggs. Spotted Sandpipers, American Woodcocks, and Ruffed Grouse may go a step further, adding a lining of soft material, often grass or leaves. Loons, grebes, cranes, and most gulls expend a little more energy in their nest construction, creating mounds from loose vegetation and other debris.

On the other hand, other birds, particularly those nesting above the ground, build considerably more ambitious structures. Over a thousand material-gathering trips can be made during the construction of a songbird nest. Despite all the effort, these nests are seldom used for more than one season, at best. Generally, only herons, raptors, and other large birds use the same nests for a number of consecutive years.

The amount of energy that a bird puts into building a nest is really a matter of need, not ambition. For many birds, nests function only as glorified egg cartons, serving to hold the clutch together. Shortly after hatching, the highly mobile and self-feeding chicks of ducks, shorebirds, and gallinaceous birds abandon their prenatal nurseries. The young of herons, raptors, hummingbirds, and songbirds are completely dependent on their parents, however, and after breaking free from their calcified prisons remain in the nest anywhere from just over a week to well over a month. Because their elevated cradles shelter helpless nestlings as well as eggs from both the elements and hungry eyes, birds with helpless (altricial) offspring invest substantially more effort and materials into nest construction than their precocial relatives.

Differences between these two general nesting strategies are also reflected in the egg structure. Precocial birds generally produce large, heavy eggs containing about 40 percent yolk. The ample supply of food along with a long incubation period (often three or four weeks) enables the young to hatch in a relatively advanced state. This is in sharp contrast to the generally small eggs of altricial birds, which contain about 25 percent yolk and yield helpless nestlings after an incubation period lasting two weeks or less. While the shorter hatch time might seem to burden altricial birds with a lighter parental load than precocial birds, an altricial nestling requires additional care in the nest for a period that often equals or even exceeds the length of the egg's incubation term. Indeed, the total time that transpires from the inception of incubation to when the young leave the nest is often not that different between altricial and precocial birds. Spotted Sandpipers and quails spend about

American Woodcocks (opposite top) and other shorebirds do not need to build substantial nests; once the young hatch, they are able to feed themselves and to run and hide if danger threatens. Eastern Kingbirds (opposite bottom) and other birds with developed nests produce helpless young that remain in the nest for a time often exceeding the length of the incubation period.

three weeks in the nest as an egg, virtually the same length of time it takes Red-winged Blackbirds and Song Sparrows to hatch, grow, and finally "fly the coup."

Regardless of how complex the nest is, its eggs require considerable attention. As optimal embryonic development occurs at temperatures of about 99 degrees Fahrenheit (37 degrees Celsius), eggs must be kept warm on cold days and cool on hot ones. Heat is transferred from the incubating bird's belly to the eggs through brood or incubation patches, exposed tracts of wrinkled, callous skin permeated with blood vessels. An incubating bird that seems to be having difficulty getting comfortable on its nest after returning from a break is just establishing proper contact between the eggs and its brood patch. The number of incubation patches varies between avian groups. Songbirds have one large central patch on the belly, while alcids (auks and puffins) have two situated toward the sides of the breast. Shorebirds, gulls, and gallinaceous birds have three: a single median and a pair of lateral brood patches. In most birds, brood patches are exposed when the overlying feathers fall out during the egg-laying period. Ducks and geese, however, can only uncover theirs by plucking out their breast feathers.

Mallard eggs take close to a month to incubate (above left), but once they hatch, the ducklings, just like (above right) the Canada Goose goslings seen here, are able to leave the nest almost immediately.

Female hummingbirds such as this Ruby-throated (below) perform all the incubation and feeding of the young. The large eggs of Killdeers (opposite) and other precocial birds contain larger amounts of yolk and require a longer incubation than the eggs of songbirds.

Not all birds possess these portable heating pads. Pelicans, cormorants, boobies, and their relatives compensate for a lack of brood patches by sitting on their eggs with their webbed feet placed on top. In Northern Gannets, the highly vascularized feet are known to transfer substantial amounts of heat into the eggs.

Hatching the eggs is usually a long, tedious affair, one in which both parents do not always participate to the same extent. In polygynous species, such as Red-winged Blackbirds and Yellow-headed Blackbirds, or in species where the males desert, as in most ducks, hummingbirds, and grouse, the females perform all the incubation duties. The tables are turned in phalaropes and other polyandrous birds, however, as it is the males that do all the brooding (perhaps in more ways than one) after being given sole custody of a clutch of eggs.

Although monogamous pairs usually share parental respon-sibilities, considerable creativity is applied to the actual division of labor. Many female songbirds, especially warblers, perform all the incubation, while the males help out by catering to their nutritional needs. In some monogamous species, nest labor is split into distinct shifts. Male Stilt Sandpipers and Mourning Doves incubate during the day, while the females keep the eggs warm at night. The night shift in woodpecker incubation is taken by the males, with both sexes taking turns during the day. European Starling pairs also share the daytime workload, but only the females incubate through the night.

The hatching of an egg, just like the birth of a mammal, ushers a new life into the outside world. A newly-hatched pre-cocial chick generally does not wait long for its siblings to share in the experience, for most clutches fully hatch in less than a day. By delaying the start of incubation until the full clutch is

(Opposite) Northern Flicker females alternate incubation duties with the males during the day but take the nights off.
Synchronous hatching of the eggs allows Canada Geese (below) and other birds with precocial offspring to bring the young to safer sites and better
feeding areas. Unlike most waterfowl, geese and swans form lifelong pair bonds and share in the parenting duties.

laid, a bird can condense the total hatching time into a matter of hours. Only a couple of hours is needed for all dozen or so eggs in a Mallard's clutch, laid over a two-week period, to hatch. Synchronized hatching is common in precocial birds as it undoubtedly offers survival benefits to the brood. By leaving the nest quickly after hatching, the chicks can scatter and hide when danger approaches. This greatly reduces the chances of a predator devouring all of them during a single visit.

Other birds begin to incubate before the last egg has been laid, with the hatch period for their full clutch spanning several days or longer. Gulls, hawks, and owls usually commence incubation after the first egg is laid, while Dark-eyed Juncos start after the third. The asynchronous hatching results in a brood of nestlings varying in size and development. This is particularly exaggerated in Barn Owl broods, where the age difference between the youngest and oldest owlet can span a full two weeks! Not uncommonly, particularly in gulls, the smallest of the brood fails to survive, often a result of starvation.

At first glance, it seems puzzling that a bird would stagger its egg hatching times when death to at least one of its young might be the result. But on closer scrutiny, asynchronous hatching may actually offer several benefits. By having a few young leave the nest early, the odds are improved that at least part of the brood might escape if a disaster were to befall the nest. Asynchronous hatching may ease the strain imposed on parents during the peak feeding period of nestlings, which is

115

The defense of eggs and young can involve dramatic distraction displays. A female Mallard will flail across the water to draw a predator's attention (opposite) while the young hide. As their chicks scurry under plants, leaves, or anything else they find, female Ruffed Grouse make themselves obvious and draw the danger away (below left). One of the most convincing acts comes from Killdeers (below right); the males in particular perform convincing broken-wing acts to lure a predator from the nest. The "bloody" rump and tail further the illusion of injury.

greatly amplified when all the young are the same age. And in times of food stress, instead of having an evenly weakened same-age brood, it is quite possible that only the youngest and smallest nestlings might perish. When starvation threatens the brood of a predatory bird, such as a Short-eared Owl, the larger chicks may even devour their smaller siblings.

Nature, in its frugality, may appear to be cruel and wasteful at times. Because eagles, cranes, and boobies usually produce two eggs that are hatched asynchronously, there is generally a great size disparity between the young birds. Frequently, the largest and strongest chick kills its smaller sibling. While this self-imposed brood reduction may seem to offer little advantage, in Black-legged Kittiwakes, for example, the frequency

of siblicide rises when food is scarce. By knocking off its competition for the scant provisions, the older chick might well be ensuring its own survival. Perhaps for long-lived birds such as cranes and eagles, raising one healthy young each year is the best strategy for long-term reproductive success. The second egg may act as an insurance policy in the event that the first fails to produce a viable young. If the first young thrives, the second becomes expendable.

Apart from those few species in which it is engrained into their reproductive cycle, siblicide is a rare phenomenon in birds. An even rarer form of brood reduction known as infanticide also occurs in some species. However, instead of the young doing each other in, it is an adult bird that kills the nestlings.

Cacti provide safe nesting sites for a few desert birds. Elf Owls (opposite, top left) will nest in vacated woodpecker cavities, while (opposite, top right) Cactus Wrens will build right among the sizable thorns. Northern Flickers (opposite, bottom left) and other woodpeckers have one of the greatest success rates of all nesting birds because they are able to make custom-sized nest holes and have impressive weapons for defense. With their fine bills, Black-capped Chickadees (opposite, bottom right) are not quite as well equipped for excavating as woodpeckers and must either use pre-made holes or excavate in punky wood.

While it might seem counter-productive, infanticide is simply a means of promoting gene transfer. When a female Tree Swallow loses her mate, an unmated male might move in and kill all her offspring. If he then pairs with the widow, she nests again and the ensuing brood carries his genes. But even if he has no eye for the widow, he can still usurp her nest site and father a brood with a female of his choosing.

Naturally, most birds vigorously defend their own nestlings against the attacks of other animals, including their own species. Defense against another creature, particularly a predator, always involves danger, so before rushing into battle a bird must weigh the potential benefits against the risks. If a nest is threatened early in the egg-laying stage, the parental reaction may seem somewhat token in comparison to the defense offered later. If only an egg or two is at risk and there is ample time for re-nesting, it really would not be prudent for a bird to risk its life. But if the breeding effort is in an advanced stage with insufficient time left for starting over, the bird would be justified in vigorously defending its young. As the nest contents increase in value as well as age, the intensity of the nest defense usually rises. But once the young reach a certain level of independence and the probability increases that they will survive, the defense antics wane. In precocial birds, the peak in nest defense occurs near egg hatching time, while in altricial birds it is nearer to the time the young fledge. In both cases, the parent birds are willing to take the greatest risk when they stand to lose the most.

If a male has full confidence in the paternity of the offspring, he is usually willing to defend them with all his vigor. But the young are not always all sired by the territorial male. When a male Red-winged Blackbird is aware of the adulterous background of his brood, he is less likely to attend to their needs. Thus, the benefits gained by a female in a neighborly encounter might well be erased by a curtailment of her mate's devotion. But for some females, "fooling around" does provide advantages for her young. Female Harris' Hawks and Acorn Woodpeckers who mate with several males benefit from a group effort in caring for their young.

Predation is one of the main causes of nest failures, but not all nest sites are equal in terms of predation risk. Remote islands are usually predator-free and nests placed high over even small bodies of water are relatively safe. Cavities that hide the eggs and young from both the environment and predators offer almost double the success of nests placed in the open. Woodpeckers and other birds who create their own cavities have even lower predation rates than those that use pre-made holes (such as Tree Swallows and bluebirds), for their entranceways are custom-fitted to their size and their weaponry is greater.

Besides predation and environmental stress, many nesting birds face yet another, rather insidious danger. When a bird leaves its nest even temporarily unguarded, there is a chance that a stranger will quickly slip in and deposit an egg into the clutch. Unless the recipient recognizes the addition as foreign, the intruder's gift will be nurtured and protected as one of its

Like a high-rise apartment, an oceanic island (below left) has tenants nesting on every possible level. Colonial seabirds
gain safety for their eggs and young, as well as quick access to food, by nesting on these remote islands.
Eastern Bluebirds (below right) have little option but to use pre-made holes and cavities for nesting. As a result, their nesting success is
considerably lower than that of an excavator, for they must take whatever cavity is available, regardless of entrance size.

own. By dropping their parental responsibilities into the nests of other birds, brood parasites successfully produce young at the expense of others.

Brood parasites vary in their dependency on others for rearing their young. Many waterfowl, including Wood Ducks, Common Goldeneyes, and Redheads (which exploit a large variety of hosts) dump an egg or two in the nests of their neighbors but also lay a full clutch in their own nest. Apart

from an occasional "adjustment" by the layer to keep the total number of eggs in the host nest the same, the donation usually has little impact on the foster mother's reproductive success. Part-time or "facultative" brood parasitism is not found only in ducks. Both Yellow-billed and Black-billed Cuckoos will "parasitize" their own species and on occasion will even "cross-lay" in the nests of each other or of other species.

The activities of a brood parasite transposed onto a human

Female Brown-headed Cowbirds (below left) escape the pressures of parenthood by dropping their eggs in the nests of other birds. If the egg is accepted (which is often the case), the foster parents will raise the cowbird as if it were one of their own. This is usually at the expense of their own young, however, for cowbirds generally hatch first and are large and demanding. In this Veery nest (below right), the cowbird nestling does not look much bigger than the thrush's nestlings, but as there are only two young Veeries instead of four, odds are the young cowbird did indeed have an impact.

situation would make a great script for a sci-fi novel or movie. Just think: "A nursery is left unguarded but for a moment. Seizing its opportunity, an alien creature slips in unnoticed. Swiftly it grabs an infant and tosses it out the window. In a flash it drops its own progeny into the vacated cradle and then vanishes as quickly as it appeared. When the matron returns, she picks up the 'new' arrival and begins to nurse it, completely unaware that the sinister switch had been made."

The egg-laying escapades of a brood parasite are indeed cut of high drama. If caught in the act, the intruder faces severe retribution by the nest owners. So, to time its break-in precisely, it must carefully monitor the residents' comings and goings. When the coast is clear, it must quickly dash in, lay its egg, and depart before being detected. The expediency in which the parasitic act is performed is astounding; many brood parasites are in and out of a host's nest in less than a

Because female ducks will often lay an egg in a neighbor's clutch, one or more of these young Common Mergansers (opposite) may not belong to the female they are with. The brood parentage might become even more mixed if another female were to dump off her young. The additional young, creating a super-sized brood known as a creche, could actually benefit a foster mother: if a predator were to strike, the odds of having all her young survive would be improved.

minute. Cliff Swallows have been clocked performing the act in as little as 15 seconds!

By not putting all its eggs in one basket, so to speak, a brood parasite potentially produces more young than it could on its own. But in an escalating race of genes, there is an evolutionary pressure on parasitized females to do unto others as others do unto them. While a female is away from her own nest on a covert mission, quite possibly some other female is back there dumping one of her eggs into the clutch.

However, not all brood parasites face the risk of retaliatory action. In North America, there are three species of birds that never make their own nests. Female Bronzed, Shiny, and Brown-headed Cowbirds have no other option but to lay in other birds' nests. These obligate brood parasites exploit the parental efforts of a great many different species; over 200 species of foster parents are known for Brown-headed Cowbird nestlings. Unlike facultative brood parasites, cowbirds are not so innocuous in their effects on their hosts. Female cowbirds often destroy one of the host's eggs, a significant loss when the full clutch may contain only four or five eggs. But for the eggs that are left to hatch, an even less savory fate awaits. Cowbird eggs hatch a day or so ahead of the hosts', and the insatiable nestlings grow quickly. Big and aggressive, young cowbirds usually outcompete the other nestlings and garner all the parents' attention. Frequently, the rightful occupants to the nest starve or are crushed by the massive charlatan. But this scenario is sometimes avoided, for a number of birds can recognize a cowbird's egg from their own and, as do

American Robins, eject it from the nest. Sometimes the nest is abandoned and a fresh clutch laid in a new nest. Yellow Warblers will even build on top of the old nest, burying the old clutch complete with the cowbird egg. As a result of these and other responses, only about three percent of all Brown-headed Cowbird eggs yield adult birds. This incredibly low success rate is offset by unusually high fecundity, however. A female cowbird can produce as many as 40 eggs in her two-month-long breeding season.

Regardless of parentage, young birds usually are protected and, if altricial, fed by their guardians. While most nestlings are cared for by two parents at the most, in a few species the young receive nurturing from one or more additional birds. Cooperative breeding or "helping" is best known in Florida Scrub Jays, Gray-breasted Jays, Groove-billed Anis, Acorn Woodpeckers, and Red-Cockaded Woodpeckers. The benefits to the helpers vary, ranging from access to a limited number of nesting territories (as in Scrub Jays) to access to clumped food resources (as in Acorn Woodpeckers). But there is always some hidden benefit to those that help. In Nature, no bird or any other animal acts solely out of the goodness of its heart.

For all birds, each and every breeding season is full of important economic decisions. Who to choose as a mate? Where to place a nest? When to desert a faltering nesting attempt? How much to risk in defense of a nestling? None of these concerns is trivial, for in the great game of life, only the successful players endure. And, for birds, true success is measured only by genetic continuance.

GLOSSARY

Afterfeather: The downy, lower portion of a contour feather.

Anting: The use of ant secretions to possibly repel fungi and bacteria in the feathers. Ants can be grabbed in the bills and passed over the feathers or can be enticed to run over the plumage when the bird squats over an ant hill.

Altricial: Young that are hatched in a helpless state.

Barbs: The parallel branches in a feather vane that arise from the rachis.

Barbules: The branches arising from the barbs that usually interlock through an opposing series of hooks and ridges.

Blade: The flat body of a feather consisting of two vanes and the rachis.

Bristle Feathers: Stiff, spike-like feathers that perform either sensory or physical functions.

Brood Patch: The exposed skin on the breast of a bird that releases heat into the eggs.

Brood Parasite: A bird that lays its eggs in the nests of other birds.

Contour Feathers: The main body covering that gives a bird its form, protects it from the elements, and allows it to fly.

Counter-Current Exchange: A heat-conservation system in the legs and feet of birds, where the arteries and veins exchange heat.

Countershading: Camouflagic coloration in which the upperparts are dark and the underside is pale. Shadows cast by the upperparts create a uniformly dark or "flat" bird.

Disruptive Coloration: Camouflagic patterns such as breast bands or eyestripes that break up or disrupt a bird's outline.

Down: Soft, fluffy feathers with hookless barbules, often covering young birds or located under other feathers.

Dusting: A method of cleaning feathers by bathing in dry soil.

Facultative Brood Parasite: A brood parasite that also maintains its own nest.

Filoplumes: Hair-like feathers that relay information to the muscles controlling feather position.

Flight Feathers: Large contour feathers lacking downy bases, located in the wings and tail.

Fovea: Retinal pits packed with sensory cells that give birds of prey superior vision.

Gallinaceous Birds: Chicken- or fowl-like birds such as grouse, quail, and turkeys.

Gape: The opening at the base of the bill.

Gizzard: A muscular stomach that grinds hard materials.

Gorget: The iridescent throat feathers of a hummingbird.

Gular Fluttering: The rapid oscillation of the throat to increase air flow through the respiratory tract. In turn, this increases the rate of evaporative cooling. Demonstrated by owls, herons, boobies, and other non-passerines.

Infanticide: The killing of young birds by adults.

Keratin: The fibrous protein that makes up leg scales and feathers.

Leks: Communal breeding grounds of Wild Turkeys and certain grouse.

Lipochromes: Feather pigments that give rise to bright colors. These can be acquired through diet.

Melanin: Feather pigmentation responsible for earth-toned colors.

Mobbing: The swarming of a predator by a group of birds.

Molt: The regular shedding and replacement of feathers.

Obligate Brood Parasite: A brood parasite that never incubates its own eggs.

Oil Gland: The gland at the upper base of the tail that provides oily secretions used in feather maintenance. Also called the preen or uropygial gland.

Parental Care: The investment of time and energy into increasing the chances of the offspring's survival at the risk of decreasing the parent's chances of producing future broods.

Passerines: Members of the Order Passeriformes — the perching birds.

Pellet: A compact ball of hair, bones, and other inedible items coughed out by owls and other predatory birds.

Polyandry: A mating system in which females have more than one mate.

Polygyny: A mating system in which males have more than one mate.

Powderdown: Special down feathers in herons that are used to waterproof feathers.

Precocial: Young that are hatched in a relatively advanced mobile and self-feeding state.

Preen Gland: *see Oil Gland*.

Preening: Feather maintenance that includes the distribution of preen gland secretions through the feathers, as well as general feather restoration and cleaning with the bill or feet.

Primary Feathers: The large wing feathers attached to the hand of the wing.

Rachis: The support shaft of a feather.

Raptor: Diurnal birds of prey, such as hawks. Some authors also consider owls to be raptors.

Rectrix (pl. **Rectrices**): A tail flight feather.

Remige: A wing flight feather.

Rete Mirabile: The intertwining network of arteries and veins in the legs of many birds that regulates heat loss.

Salt Gland: A large nasal gland for removing salt from seawater. Found in seabirds such as fulmars and petrels.

Scapulars: Feathers arising from the shoulders.

Semiplumes: Insulating feathers intermediate in structure between contour and down feathers. Occasionally elaborated into display plumes.

Sexual Selection: The evolutionary force driven by selection between the sexes and aggression within a sex. This selection pressure gives rise to appearances and behaviors associated only with mating.

Siblicide: The killing of a young bird by its sibling.

Speculum: The iridescent wing patch of a duck.

Torpor: An energy-efficient state of induced hypothermia in which a bird's temperature and metabolism drop.

Uropygial Gland: *see Oil Gland*.

Vane: In a feather, the parts of the flat blade that lie on either side of the rachis.

ADDITIONAL READING

Today we live in an age in which the "whats" are being replaced by the "hows" and the "whys." A very active body of research is currently being conducted on birds around the world. To learn about recent findings, scientific journals such as *Animal Behaviour*, *American Naturalist*, *Auk*, *Condor*, and *Behavioural Ecology and Sociobiology* — to name only a few — should be perused. Numerous excellent overviews of specific aspects of avian biology are also available (several are listed below), and new ones come into being almost annually. These publications contain the specific references that will guide you to the original research papers.

An excellent source of current information about birds is the ongoing series *Current Ornithology* (Plenum Press, New York, NY). In addition, it is hoped that the following publications will open the doors to the vast and constantly growing world of literature concerning our amazing birds.

Alerstam, T. *Bird Migration*. New York, NY: Cambridge University Press, 1990.

Andersson, M. *Sexual Selection*. Princeton, NJ: Princeton University Press, 1994.

Berthold, P. Bird *Migration: A General Survey*. New York, NY: Oxford University Press, 1993.

Birkhead, T. R., and A. P. Moller. *Sperm Competition in Birds: Evolutionary Causes and Consequences*. San Diego, CA: Academic Press, 1992.

Clutton-Brock, T. H. *The Evolution of Parental Care*. Princeton, NJ: Princeton University Press, 1991.

Ehrlich, P. R., D. S. Dobkin, and D. Wheye. *The Birder's Handbook: A Field Guide to the Natural History of North American Birds*. New York, NY: Simon and Schuster, 1988.

Gill, F. B. *Ornithology*, 2nd ed. New York, NY: W. H. Freeman and Company, 1994.

Howe, H. F., and L. C. Westley. *Ecological Relationships of Plants and Animals*. New York, NY: Oxford University Press, 1988.

Krebs, J. R., and N. B. Davies. *An Introduction to Behavioural Ecology*, 3rd ed. New York, NY: Blackwell Scientific Publications, 1993.

Snow, B. and D. *Birds and Berries*. London, GB: T & AD Poyser, 1988.

Terres, J. K., ed. *The Encyclopedia of North American Birds*. New York, NY: Alfred A. Knopf, 1980.

Welty, J. C. *The Life of Birds*, 3rd ed. New York, NY: Saunders, 1982.

PHOTO CREDITS

MICHAEL RUNTZ

Front cover, 2, 8, 11, 12, 17 (upper left, upper right), 18, 22, 24, 28, 29, 32, 33, 35, 36, 37, 38, 41, 42, (left), 43, 44, 47, 49, 50, 51, 56, 57, 61 (lower), 70, 71, 72 (lower right), 74, 75, 77 (right), 78, 81, 84, 85 (upper), 87, 92, 94, 96, 97, 99 (upper right), 101, 104, 106, 107, 109, 110, 111, 112 (left), 113, 114, 115, 116, 117, 119 (lower right), 120, 121 (right), 123, back cover (upper left, lower right).

JIM FLYNN

6, 13, 15, 17 (lower), 19, 21, 23, 25, 26, 27, 31, 39, 40, 42 (right), 45, 53, 54, 55, 59, 61 (upper), 62, 63, 65, 66, 67, 68, 69, 72 (upper left, upper right, lower left), 73, 77 (left), 79, 82, 83, 85 (lower), 88, 89, 90, 91, 93, 95, 99 (upper left, lower left, lower right), 103, 105, 112 (right), 119 (upper left, upper right, lower left), 121 (left), back cover (lower left, upper right).

INDEX